# Censorship

### An OPPOSING  VIEWPOINTS® Guide

Lauri S. Friedman, *Book Editor*

**OPPOSING
VIEWPOINTS®
SERIES**

**GREENHAVEN PRESS**
*A part of Gale, Cengage Learning*

 GALE
CENGAGE Learning™

Detroit • New York • San Francisco • New Haven, Conn • Waterville, Maine • London

Christine Nasso, Publisher
Elizabeth Des Chenes, Managing Editor

For more information, contact:
Greenhaven Press
27500 Drake Rd.
Farmington Hills, MI 48331-3535
Or you can visit our Internet site at http://gale.cengage.com

For product information and technology assistance, contact us at

Gale Customer Support, 1-800-877-4253
For permission to use material from this text or product, submit all requests online at www.cengage.com/permissions

Further permissions questions can be emailed to permissionrequest@cengage.com

Articles in Greenhaven Press anthologies are often edited for length to meet page requirements. In addition, original titles of these works are changed to clearly present the main thesis and to explicitly indicate the author's opinion. Every effort is made to ensure that Greenhaven Press accurately reflects the original intent of the authors. Every effort has been made to trace the owners of copyrighted material.

Cover image Keith Philpott/Time Life Pictures/Getty Images

**LIBRARY OF CONGRESS CATALOGING-IN-PUBLICATION DATA**

Censorship / Lauri S. Friedman, book editor.
    p. cm. — (Writing the critical essay : an opposing viewpoints guide)
Includes bibliographical references and index.
 ISBN 978-0-7377-4401-9 (hardcover)
1. Censorship—United States. 2. Freedom of speech—United States.
3. Essay—Authorship—Problems, exercises, etc. 4. Rhetoric—Problems, exercises, etc. I. Friedman, Lauri S.
 Z658.U5C3925 2009
 363.310973—dc22
                                                     2008055429

Printed in the United States of America
1 2 3 4 5 6 7 13 12 11 10 09

# CONTENTS

## Section Three: Supporting Research Material

Examining the state of writing and how it is taught in the United States was the official purpose of the National Commission on Writing in America's Schools and Colleges. The commission, made up of teachers, school administrators, business leaders, and college and university presidents, released its first report in 2003. "Despite the best efforts of many educators," commissioners argued, "writing has not received the full attention it deserves." Among the findings of the commission was that most fourth-grade students spent less than three hours a week writing, that three-quarters of high school seniors never receive a writing assignment in their history or social studies classes, and that more than 50 percent of first-year students in college have problems writing error-free papers. The commission called for a "cultural sea change" that would increase the emphasis on writing for both elementary and secondary schools. These conclusions have made some educators realize that writing must be emphasized in the curriculum. As colleges are demanding an ever-higher level of writing proficiency from incoming students, schools must respond by making students more competent writers. In response to these concerns, the SAT, an influential standardized test used for college admissions, required an essay for the first time in 2005.

Books in the Writing the Critical Essay: An Opposing Viewpoints Guide series use the patented Opposing Viewpoints format to help students learn to organize ideas and arguments and to write essays using common critical writing techniques. Each book in the series focuses on a particular type of essay writing—including expository, persuasive, descriptive, and narrative—that students learn while being taught both the five-paragraph essay as well as longer pieces of writing that have an opinionated focus. These guides include everything necessary to help students research, outline, draft, edit, and ultimately write successful essays across the curriculum, including essays for the SAT.

## Using Opposing Viewpoints

This series is inspired by and builds upon Greenhaven Press's acclaimed Opposing Viewpoints series. As in the parent series, each book in the Writing the Critical Essay series focuses on a timely and controversial social issue that provides lots of opportunities for creating thought-provoking essays. The first section of each volume begins with a brief introductory essay that provides context for the opposing viewpoints that follow. These articles are chosen for their accessibility and clearly stated views. The thesis of each article is made explicit in the article's title and is accentuated by its pairing with an opposing or alternative view. These essays are both models of persuasive writing techniques and valuable research material that students can mine to write their own informed essays. Guided reading and discussion questions help lead students to key ideas and writing techniques presented in the selections.

The second section of each book begins with a preface discussing the format of the essays and examining characteristics of the featured essay type. Model five-paragraph and longer essays then demonstrate that essay type. The essays are annotated so that key writing elements and techniques are pointed out to the student. Sequential, step-by-step exercises help students construct and refine thesis statements; organize material into outlines; analyze and try out writing techniques; write transitions, introductions, and conclusions; and incorporate quotations and other re-searched material. Ultimately, students construct their own compositions using the designated essay type.

The third section of each volume provides additional research material and writing prompts to help the student. Additional facts about the topic of the book serve as a convenient source of supporting material for essays. Other features help students go beyond the book for their research. Like other Greenhaven Press books, each book in the Writing the Critical Essay series includes bibliographic listings of relevant periodical articles, books, Web sites, and organizations to contact.

Writing the Critical Essay: An Opposing Viewpoints Guide will help students master essay techniques that can be used in any discipline.

# E-Censorship

Censorship is a problem nearly as old as America itself: This is why the right to free speech was granted in the First Amendment of the Bill of Rights. Since 1791, when Americans were guaranteed that Congress would make no law abridging their freedom of speech, people have hotly debated whether pornography, flag burning, obscene language, and other forms of expression should be constitutionally protected as free speech. In the twenty-first century, debates over free speech and censorship have shifted to the newest medium of communication: the Internet. Particularly, pro–eating disorder Web sites, otherwise known as "pro-ana" (short for *anorexia*) and "pro-mia" (short for *bulimia*) sites, have come under scrutiny as being candidates for censorship. Such sites glorify and idolize thin celebrities, offer advice on how to conceal eating-disordered behaviors, and applaud unhealthy weight loss.

Critics claim that pro-ana and pro-mia sites should be shut down because they rationalize and encourage a very serious and potentially deadly disease. They argue that while many sites operate under the pretense of providing a supportive, educational environment, they do little more than fuel an individual's desire to remain eating disordered, or to develop the disorder. Indeed, sites that teach bulimics to cover the sound of vomiting by turning on the shower or keep their fingernails painted bright colors to hide telltale signs of induced vomiting reinforce unhealthy behaviors and reduce the likelihood that an individual will seek help for his or her problem.

Recovering anorexic Jill Meredith Collins is one person who believes pro–eating disorder sites must be censored because of the threat they pose to young people. Writes Collins of eating disorder sufferers who visit pro-ana sites, "They do not get the help they need from the pro-anorexia websites: instead they get reinforcement of the problem that they want to overcome. In that stage, it's very difficult to overcome something when others are convincing you that you don't need to."[1] Because anorexia and bulimia can permanently alter a young person's body and result in coma and death, Collins and others argue sites that promote such self-harm should be shut down.

Furthermore, because pro–eating disorder Web sites are usually run by young women who suffer from eating

*In the twenty-first century, free speech and censorship have been hotly debated. Some express the right to free speech by protests, flag burning, or symbolic demonstrations such as putting tape over one's mouth.*

# How Different Countries Rate Freedom of the Press

A 2007 survey of 11,344 people in fourteen countries revealed a world divided about the importance of free speech in the press. Overall, 56 percent of those interviewed thought that freedom of the press was very important to ensure a free society. But 40 percent said it was more important to maintain social harmony and peace, even if it meant curbing the press's freedom to report news truthfully.

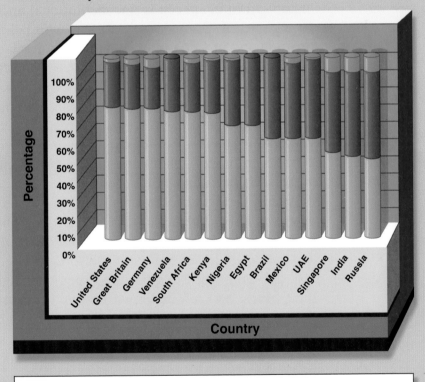

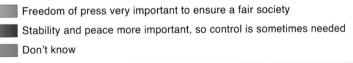

Freedom of press very important to ensure a fair society

Stability and peace more important, so control is sometimes needed

Don't know

Taken from: BBC World Service/GlobeScan/Synovate, 2007.

disorders themselves, it is feared they prey upon young teenagers who are already insecure about their rapidly changing bodies. Indeed, teenagers undergoing puberty are among the more peer-pressure-sensitive sectors of society. This was the experience of one teenager who developed an eating disorder after visiting pro-ana sites. "The more time I spent browsing these 'pro-ana' Web sites, the more I began to criticize myself. I could see all of my own flaws: my flabby thighs, my chubby cheeks, everything is ugly," she said. "How could I feel good about myself when everything online told me I was too fat?"[2]

But others have fought against the censorship of pro–eating disorder Web sites on the grounds that censoring any form of speech is unconstitutional and morally wrong. Gracie Doran is one person who believes that pro-ana and pro-mia Web sites have as much of a right to exist as any other site on the Internet. "We cannot choose what can be put on the Internet and what can't," argues Doran. "Right or wrong, this information is out there. Be aware that, like most things, not everything you find on the Internet should be taken with you."[3] For Doran and others, what content to view online should be a user's decision—not a censor's.

And in fact, such Web sites might not be as harmful as critics have claimed. In fact, a 2007 study published in the journal *Eating Disorders: The Journal of Treatment and Prevention* found that eating-disorder sufferers who visit pro-ana Web sites do so to seek connection with their peers, and as such often end up seeking support and recovery. While many users do suffer as a result of looking at the sites, others find them to be a comforting, safe, judgment-free place where they can discuss their feelings with people who can empathize. Indeed, visitors to pro-ana and pro-mia sites say they have few real-world resources to help them deal with their eating disorder; as a result, they turn to the online community for precious support. "Once accepted by the community, members often showed themselves to be fiercely loyal and encouraging," found study authors Sarah R. Brotsky and David Giles. "A general sense of support is the central function of pro-ana sites."[4] For this reason, Brotsky and Giles concluded that pro–eating disorder Web sites provide a safe harbor for those seeking help for an eating disorder and argue "it is difficult to claim that pro-ana sites encourage non-eating-disordered people to become eating disordered."[5] From this perspective, then, censoring pro-ana and pro-mia sites is not only unnecessary but

*Free speech and censorship continue to be powerful issues in the digital era.*

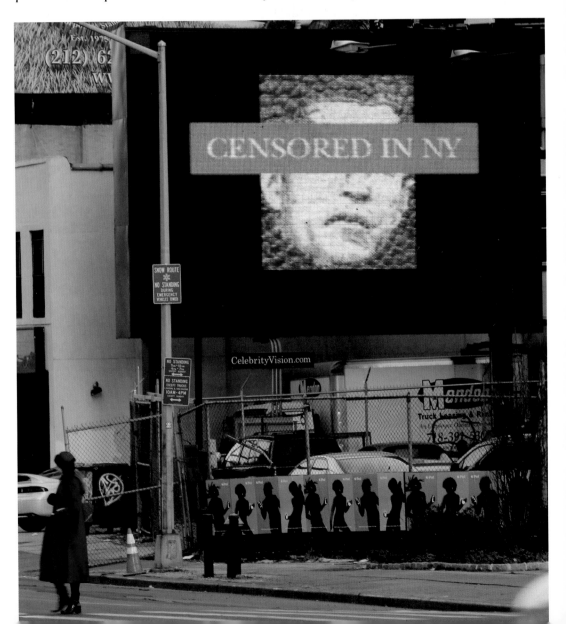

# Censorship in America

Each year on the anniversary of Thomas Jefferson's birthday, the Thomas Jefferson Center, an organization devoted to the defense of free speech, publishes a list of persons, groups, or entities it claims showed a flagrant disregard for fundamental First Amendment principles. In 2008 it named the following individuals or organizations as the worst offenders:

**Bush Administration (Washington, DC)**

For discouraging, changing, and sometimes censoring the reports and studies of government scientists in order to make them more supportive of political policies.

**The National Collegiate Athletic Association (Indianapolis, IN)**

For selectively imposing a policy prohibiting the use by collegiate teams of Native American names, mascots, and symbols.

**The Philadelphia Commission on Human Relations (Philadelphia, PA)**

For filing a discrimination complaint against Geno's Steaks on the basis of the public display of a sign reading "This Is America . . . When Ordering, Speak English."

**United States Department of Defense (Arlington, VA)**

For launching and sustaining a program, ostensibly aimed at counterterrorism, that gathered and stored information about antiwar demonstrators and other citizen groups that posed no obvious national security threat.

**The Maine Bureau of Liquor Enforcement (Augusta, ME)**

For denying a beer distributor's application to sell three beers in the state because it disapproved of the artwork on the beers' labels.

**The Federal Communications Commission (Washington, DC)**

For broadening the scope of broadcast material that may constitute forbidden "indecency" and for targeting alleged "profanity."

**U.S. Representative Peter King (Albany, NY)**

For calling on the Justice Department to seek criminal sanctions against a newspaper and its staff for disclosing publicly the existence and extent of covert, warrantless surveillance by the National Security Administration.

**The City Council of East St. Louis, Illinois (East St. Louis, IL)**

For canceling the contract with the owner of a public access television station because he criticized city council policies on air.

**The Miami-Dade County School Board (Miami, FL)**

For attempting to remove children's picture books from school libraries because the books were not sufficiently critical of life in Cuba under the Castro regime.

**The Administration of Kentucky Governor Ernie Fletcher (Frankfort, KY)**

For selectively blocking the workplace access of state employees to certain political blogs and other Internet sites that had posted statements critical of the governor and his administration.

**Wyoming Valley West High School (Kingston, PA)**

For censoring the content of high school publications.

**The Ohio General Assembly (Columbus, OH)**

For requiring, under the Ohio PATRIOT Act, that all applicants for employment with the state of Ohio or any of its agencies must answer satisfactorily six intrusive and ambiguous questions pertaining to political beliefs and activities.

Taken from: The Thomas Jefferson Center, 2008.

could remove a critical support network that could lead to recovery for some eating-disorder sufferers.

Efforts to censor pro–eating disorder sites have been met with mixed results. After the National Association of Anorexia Nervosa and Associated Disorders (ANAD) informed Yahoo! about their presence and potential threat, the company removed pro-ana sites from its Yahoo! Groups platform on the grounds that the sites advocated self-harm and were in violation of Yahoo!'s terms of use. More sites were shut down in 2007 when Microsoft eliminated four pro-ana sites that were hosted on a Spanish networking service.

The networking groups Facebook and MySpace, however, have refused to censor the sites of pro–eating disorder groups. A spokesperson for MySpace explained that in addition to being a violation of the First Amendment, it is often difficult to tell the difference between genuine eating disorder support groups and groups that might be pro-ana, and to shut them all down seems unfair and unproductive. "Rather than censor these groups, we are working to create partnerships with organizations"[6] that can provide help to eating disorder sufferers, explained a MySpace spokesperson. Facebook, too, has resisted calls to shut down pro-ana groups, arguing, "Many Facebook groups relate to controversial topics; this alone is not a reason to disable a group."[7] And even when such sites are censored, it does not seem to stop them from existing. According to Optenet, a global IT security company, the number of Web sites that promote anorexia and bulimia has increased a whopping 470 percent since 2006. Clearly, censorship efforts have not prevented their expansion, a fact that opponents of censorship cite when they urge people to leave the sites alone.

The censorship of pro–eating disorder Web sites is just one topic debated in *Writing the Critical Essay: Censorship*. Students will also read viewpoints and model essays that discuss what kinds of speech should be censored, what the consequences of censorship are, and how the First Amendment should be interpreted. Model essays and viewpoints expose readers to the basic arguments made about censorship and help them develop tools to craft their own expository essays on the subject.

## Notes

1. Jill Meredith Collins, "Nurturing Destruction: Eating Disorders Online," *Off Our Backs*, vol. 34, nos. 11/12, November-December 2004, p. 21.

2. Quoted in *L.A. Youth*, "How Thin Do I Have to Be?" September 2005, p. 10.

3. Gracie Doran, "Everything Online Should Not Be Digested," *Daily Evergreen*, July 13, 2006. www.daily evergreen.com/story/18243.

4. Sarah R. Brotsky and David Giles, "Inside the 'Pro-ana' Community: A Covert Online Participant Observation," *Eating Disorders: The Journal of Treatment and Prevention*, vol. 15, no. 2, March 2007, pp. 93–109.

5. Brotsky and Giles, "Inside the 'Pro-ana' Community," pp. 93–109.

6. Quoted in British Broadcasting Service, "Pro-anorexia Site Clampdown Urged," February 24, 2008. http://news.bbc.co.uk/2/hi/health/7259143.stm.

7. Quoted in British Broadcasting Service, "Pro-anorexia Site Clampdown Urged."

# Section One: Opposing Viewpoints on Censorship

# Terrorist Speech Should Be Censored

## Newt Gingrich

In the following essay Newt Gingrich argues the words and ideas of terrorists should not be protected under the First Amendment. He reminds Americans that not all speech is protected as free speech under the Constitution and argues that the document that founded America and gave citizens their most precious rights should not be used as a shield to protect terrorists and murderers. He suggests that Web sites that espouse terrorism be shut down and the First Amendment be altered to make sure it cannot be used to protect America's enemies. Gingrich concludes that terrorists and others who would do harm to America do not deserve to have their words and ideas protected by the Constitution.

Gingrich is the former Speaker of the U.S. House of Representatives and author of *Winning the Future*.

## Consider the following questions:

1. According to the author, what kind of speech does the First Amendment not protect?
2. Describe the "Geneva-like convention" the author proposes establishing and how it relates to his argument.
3. Who are the "flying Imams"?

I must have hit a nerve.

In New Hampshire last week [by November 2006], at a dinner hosted by the Loeb School honoring our 1st-Amendment rights, I called for a serious debate about the 1st Amendment and how terrorists are abusing our

Newt Gingrich, "The 1st Amendment Is Not a Suicide Pact: Blocking the Speech That Calls for Our Death," *Human Events*, December 4, 2006. Reproduced by permission.

rights—using them as they once used passenger jets—to threaten and kill Americans.

Here's part of what I said: "Either before we lose a city, or, if we are truly stupid, after we lose a city, we will adopt rules of engagement that use every technology we can find to break up [terrorists'] capacity to use the Internet, to break up their capacity to use free speech [protections] and to go after people who want to kill us—to stop them from recruiting people before they get to reach out and convince young people to destroy their lives while destroying us."

*Members of the "six Imams" speak to the press following their removal from an airplane for allegedly acting suspiciously on the plane.*

## Free Speech Is Not an Acceptable Cover for Those Planning to Kill

Since I made those remarks, I've heard from many, many Americans who understand the seriousness of the threat that faces us, Americans who believe as I do that free speech should not be an acceptable cover for people who are planning to kill other people who have inalienable rights of their own.

A small number of others have been quick to demagogue my remarks. Missing from the debate? Any reference to the very real threats that face Americans.

There was no mention of last week's letter from Iranian leader [Mahmoud] Ahmadinejad that threatens to kill Americans in large numbers if we don't submit to his demands.

There has been little attention drawn to any of the many websites dedicated to training and recruiting terrorists, including a recent one that promises to train terrorists "to use the Internet for the sake of jihad."

No mention of efforts by terrorist groups like Hezbollah to build "franchises" among leftist, anti-globalization groups worldwide, especially in Latin America.

## Words as Weapons

The fact is not all speech is permitted under the Constitution. The 1st Amendment does not protect lewd and libelous speech, and it should not—and cannot in 2006—be used as a shield for murderers.

Former federal prosecutor Andy McCarthy put it best: "With an enemy committed to terrorism, the advocacy of terrorism—the threats, the words—are not mere dogma, or even calls to 'action.' They are themselves weapons—weapons of incitement and intimidation, often as effective in achieving their ends as would be firearms and explosives brandished openly."

We need a serious dialogue—not knee-jerk hysteria—about the 1st Amendment, what it protects and what it should not protect. Here are a few baseline principles to consider:

## Restrictions on Terrorist Speech

- We should be allowed to close down websites that recruit suicide bombers and provide instructions to indiscriminately kill civilians by suicide or other means, or advocate killing people from the West or the destruction of Western civilization;
- We should propose a Geneva-like convention for fighting terrorism that makes very clear that those who would fight outside the rules of law, those who would use weapons of mass destruction and those who would target civilians are in fact subject to a totally different set of rules that allow us to protect civilization by defeating barbarism before it gains so much strength that it is truly horrendous. A subset of this convention should define the international rules of engagement on what activities will not be protected by free speech claims; and
- We need an expeditious review of current domestic law to see what changes can be made within the protections of the 1st Amendment to ensure that free speech protection claims are not used to protect the advocacy of terrorism, violent conduct or the killing of innocents.

## Letting Our Freedom and Tolerance Be Used Against Us

And just as free-speech protections shouldn't be allowed to shield activities that threaten Americans, so too should we not allow our great national belief in nondiscrimination and equality before the law to be used against us.

Indications are growing that this is precisely what the group of Islamic clerics who were removed from a US Airways flight [on November 20, 2006] was engaged in: an effort to intimidate our airlines and air security officials into tolerating suspicious behavior for fear of being labeled a bigot—or worse.

Recall that the six Imams were removed from a US Airways flight from Minneapolis to Phoenix after exhibiting suspicious behavior. They quickly produced a lawyer who argued that their rights had been violated and news reports were quick to assert that the airline had acted improperly.

## Mimicking the September 11 Hijackers

But consider these facts, which are slowly coming to light via bloggers and independent voices in the mainstream media:

- Although the men all boarded the plane together, they spread out once they were inside—as if mim-

*Newt Gingrich argues that not all speech is permitted under the Constitution, and it does not protect lewd and libelous speech.*

icking the 9/11 hijackers—two in the front of the plane, two in the middle and two in the rear. According to the airline, some took seats not assigned to them.

- An Arabic speaker seated near the two in the rear of the plane reported that the men were invoking "bin Laden" and condemning America for "killing Saddam."
- Several of the Imams asked for seat-belt extenders, even though they did not appear to need them.

Not just one passenger (as had been reported) but multiple people on the plane and in the airport prior to boarding reported that the group of men was acting suspiciously.

Writing in the *New York Post*, Richard Miniter reports that, contrary to reports that the airline acted precipitously or singled anyone out for "flying while Muslim," the captain of the flight consulted several sources—including a federal air marshal—before making the decision to remove the Imams. All agreed that the men were behaving suspiciously.

As more and more information comes to light, it's becoming clear that US Airways should be commended for the fair and professional manner in which it handled this situation.

## We Cannot Help Those Who Want to Hurt Us

Congress should pass a resolution making it clear that we will not tolerate those who seek to intimidate us into relaxing our security procedures. Troublemakers like the six in Minneapolis should be arrested and prosecuted

## Using Free Speech Against Us

Islamist terrorist organizations use YouTube to disseminate their propaganda, enlist followers, and provide weapons training—activities that are all essential to terrorist activity. . . . I ask you, therefore, to immediately remove content produced by Islamist terrorist organizations from YouTube.

Committee on Homeland Security and Governmental Affairs, "Lieberman Calls on Google to Take Down Terrorist Content," May 19, 2008. http://hsgac.senate.gov/public/index.cfm?Fuseaction=PressReleases.Detail&PressRelease_id=8093d5b2-c882-4d12-883d-5c670d43d269 &Month-5& Year-2008.

—both for the security of the flying public and as a deterrent to future provocative acts. The message must go out: We are a fair and tolerant nation. But we will not allow our tolerance to be used as a weapon against us.

The "flying Imams," it now seems clear, were testing us. We should let them and everyone else watching know that we passed.

## Analyze the essay:

1. To make his argument, Gingrich tells the story of the flying Imams, six men who were removed from a US Airways flight after behaving suspiciously. Do you agree with Gingrich that the men were justly removed from the flight?

2. Gingrich raises the point that in the war on terror, words are weapons. Explain in detail what he means by this. Do you agree or disagree? How does this influence your opinion on whether the speech of terrorists should be protected?

# Terrorist Speech Should Not Be Censored

## American Press Institute

Founded by newspaper publishers in 1946, the American Press Institute (API) is devoted to training and professional development for the news industry and journalism educators. In the following essay members of API argue that although it is tempting to censor the words and thoughts of terrorists, they should be allowed to express themselves without regulation. The authors argue it is impossible to make judgments about which speech is acceptable and which is not. If terrorist-related speech is banned, nothing can prevent other unpopular ideas from being suppressed, which the authors say would be a critical blow to democracy and American values. Furthermore, banning hate speech does not eradicate hate—in fact, the authors suggest it might have the opposite effect, arguing that hate speech and hate tend to flourish when they are punished or made taboo. The authors conclude that if Americans want to truly silence terrorists, they must counter their hateful words and ideas with stronger, nobler, and more inspirational ones, rather than with censorship.

## Consider the following questions:

1. How might banning terrorist speech pose a problem for journalists, scholars, and political analysts, according to the authors?
2. What do the authors suggest is the correct way to deal with "bad speech"?
3. What do the authors say hate speech exposes about the people who speak it?

American Press Institute, "Criminalizing Terrorist Speech Is Tempting but Wrong," americanpressinstitute.org, January 6, 2005. Reproduced by permission.

Should Americans tolerate the invective flung at them by terrorists or their supporters, speech that is not just offensive or hateful but downright scary?

## Tempting but Wrong

[Scholar and writer] Bruce Fein doesn't think so. He does not believe there should be a haven in our free-speech traditions for "hate speech teaching that indiscriminate murders are morally justified to further a crazed reli-

*Though conservative constitutional attorney Bruce Fein makes a strong argument for criminalizing terrorist speech, the American Press Institute disagrees and believes that terrorists should be allowed to express themselves without regulation.*

gious, racial, ethnic or political cause.'' Fein believes there is a direct line from such speech to acts of terrorism, and he wants this speech outlawed.

Bruce Fein is not just some pundit on a rant. He is a constitutional scholar and an estimable thinker. And in a recent article in *The Washington Times*, he makes a strong argument for the criminalization of terrorist speech. "Freedom of speech does not include expression that hopes to provoke violence in order to destroy democracy, the rule of law or human rights," he contends.

Our first instinct, of course, is to agree with Fein wholeheartedly. Why should we endure speech that crackles with a bitter desire for our destruction?

But we should not follow our initial instincts on a matter of such consequence. Any attempt to criminalize so-called hate speech, even that of the terrorist, is unwise, unworkable and unconstitutional.

## Impossible to Draw the Line

From a practical point of view, drafting a law that narrowly targets "terrorist speech" would be a task fraught with futility. Precision and fairness would be elusive. For example, Fein would include "advocacy of jihad" in language to be banned, yet "jihad" is a broad term used in many different ways.

And it is next to impossible to come up with a definition that would confine the law's application to its intended target. Expanding the definition to include the hateful speech of racists, anti-abortionists, homophobes, white supremacists and others would be tempting.

Distinguishing terrorist speech from the work of journalists, scholars and political analysts presents another hurdle. Would such a law, for example, prevent news organizations from reporting Osama bin Laden's latest dispatch from his hideout?

Similar attempts to criminalize hate speech, whether for racial or sexist expression, have been ruled unconstitutional by federal courts.

## Hate Speech Tends to Flourish When It Is Punished

But even if such a law could be drafted, even if its reach could be extended beyond our borders, where most such speech originates, it still would not solve the problem. We know from experience that a series of international covenants and hate-speech laws in several countries have failed to stop either the speech or the hate. To our dismay, it flourishes, even where it is illegal and punished severely.

Aside from the legal problems, there is the problem of logic. For example, Fein concedes that no one knows for sure what causes terrorist acts and that the link between speech and action is tenuous at best. There is a real danger in proposing to regulate speech, let alone punish it, based on mere assertions of a connection between speech and violence rather than a certainty.

Finally, there is the challenge such a proposal poses to our democratic values. We should not let advocates of violence stampede us into a flight from our principles, to slight the idea of a free society in our quest for a more secure society.

> ## Free Speech Can Help Fight Terrorism
>
> Unfettered access to a free Internet is not merely a goal to which we should aspire on principle, but also a very practical means of countering Al Qaeda. As users increasingly make themselves heard, the ensuing chaos will not be to everyone's liking, but it may shake the online edifice of Al Qaeda's totalitarian ideology.
>
> Daniel Kimmage, "Free Speech Undermines Terrorism," *International Herald Tribune*, July 2, 2008. http://armiesofliberation.com/archives/2008/07/02/free-speech-undermines-terrorism.

## Democracies Tolerate *All* Speech, Not *Some*

Criminalizing political advocacy, even odious advocacy, is one of the most pernicious forms of censorship. It is not a shield against offensive or violent speech but a double-edged sword that hacks away at vital protections for all freedoms. That is why—with some regrettable exceptions—Americans routinely decline to make a distinction between so-called "acceptable" speech and

that which offends, or harms, or even scares us when deciding on First Amendment protections.

And that is why a series of Supreme Court opinions and two centuries of shared experience come down solidly on the side of the idea that the answer to bad speech is good speech, not censorship.

*Supreme Court rulings over the past two centuries have backed the idea that the answer to bad speech is good speech, not censorship.*

## Banning Hate Speech Does Not Get Rid of Hate

Banning speech about hate, after all, does not eliminate hate or violence. But it may eliminate a fundamental freedom—and illuminate the fragility of Americans' attachment to all other freedoms.

Even if we had the power or the ability to censor the language used in Islamic schools, textbooks and mosques, as Fein suggests, should we? Is that who we are? Is that what we stand for?

As much as we worry about the possibility that terrorist speech may incite violence against us, we must resist the temptation to criminalize such utterances. We should focus instead on the fact that hate speech exposes the haters for what they are, for their ignorance, their fear, their irrationality and occasionally their intent.

Instead, when we respond to such speech by affirming our own values, we demonstrate to the world—including those the terrorists would like to turn against us—the strength of our commitment to the tolerance of intolerance and the vital function of freedom of speech in protecting freedom for all.

## Analyze the essay:

1. The American Press Institute argues that one reason terrorist speech should not be banned is the lack of evidence that such speech actually causes or encourages violence. How would Newt Gingrich, the author of the previous essay, respond to this argument?

2. Newt Gingrich and the American Press Institute offer opposing views on the limits of free speech and what ideas and thoughts are protected under the First Amendment. After reading both essays, with which perspective do you agree? Say whether you think terrorist speech should be banned or not, and explain how you came to your conclusion.

# The Internet Should Be Censored

Peter Grad

In the following essay Peter Grad argues that the Internet should be censored. Grad discusses how video sites such as YouTube have allowed videos of terrorists beheading innocent people and child suicide bombers to be posted. In Grad's opinion, these images do not contribute to any healthy community debate, nor are they the reflection of a credible organization's respectable values. As such, they are not protected by the First Amendment. Grad says that Americans are confused about the nature of free speech. He says that merely saying *something* is not grounds for it to be protected or tolerated—this is why the thoughts, words, and ideas of child molesters, rapists, traders of national secrets, and others are not granted free speech's protection. Likewise, people who murder innocents do not deserve to have their thoughts broadcast on the Internet. Grad urges lawmakers and commentators to abide by reasonable requests to remove such images from the Internet, arguing that senseless violence should not be allowed to hide behind free speech.

## Consider the following questions:

1. What did Senator Joseph Lieberman ask of Google, as reported by the author?
2. What is Ansar al-Islam?
3. What are two examples the author gives of how YouTube has been inconsistent in its decency standards?

Peter Grad, "Terrorists Videos Don't Belong on YouTube," *The Record* (Bergen County, NJ), May 31, 2008, p. F8. Copyright © 2008 *The Record* (Bergen Co., NJ), Peter Grad. Reproduced by permission.

Peter Grad is known as "the PC Guy." He writes a weekly column in the e-living section of the *Record*, a North New Jersey newspaper from which this essay is taken.

*Senator Joe Lieberman stirred controversy when he asked Google to remove terrorist-sponsored videos from its video-sharing Web site, YouTube.*

I've not been a big fan of Sen. Joseph Lieberman since I voted for [former vice president and presidential candidate Al] Gore and him in 2000, his gushing support for the president's course in Iraq a key, though not the sole, factor.

But I think the senator is getting a bad rap on a recent dust-up concerning the Internet and the issue of free speech. Lieberman recently wrote to Google, which owns

the popular video-sharing site YouTube, asking that it remove videos sponsored by terrorist organizations.

His request seemed reasonable enough.

## A Reasonable Request

"A great majority of these videos document horrific attacks on American soldiers in Iraq or Afghanistan," the senator said. Others detail weapons-training procedures to be used against enemies of the radical groups.

But he has drawn criticism in some quarters, including the *New York Times*, which slammed Lieberman in an editorial last week. It declared Lieberman a "censor" who is attempting to "demonize" the Internet, and found it "profoundly disturbing" that he would "consider telling a media company to shut down constitutionally protected speech."

The *Times'* confusion over censorship aside Lieberman merely asked Google to observe its own guidelines against offensive materials; there were no threats or order. The newspaper's notion of propriety in this case is troubling.

## Beheadings, Attacks Are Not Free Speech

Lieberman pointed to the appearance of dozens of videos housed on YouTube that are sponsored by terrorist organizations such as al-Qaida and Ansar al-Islam. These are not neighborhood benevolent associations or book discussion clubs. These organizations engage in violent, random destruction aimed at largely innocent victims. They recruit children to wear explosives and blow up themselves and others of the "wrong" religion or political persuasion. They have instigated massacres, and Ansar al-Islam has been tied to the beheadings of 53 villagers.

The *Times* and YouTube would have us believe that these videos are merely part of a community debate. Too often, well-intentioned folks reflexively reach for the First Amendment when talk about the boundaries of speech is raised. It sounds nice to utter the words free speech and embrace the wonderful notion that however extreme the sentiments, the marketplace of ideas will nourish the sound ones and dispense with the poor ones.

## Americans Want Internet Regulation

A 2008 poll of American adults found that the majority support some form of Internet regulation.

*Question: Should the Federal Communications Commission regulate the Internet like it does radio and television?*

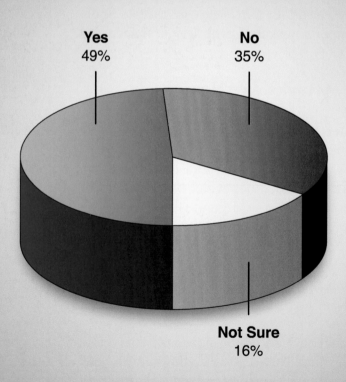

**Yes**
49%

**No**
35%

**Not Sure**
16%

Taken from: Rasmussen Reports, June, 16–17, 2008.

Such absolutists say, as the *Times* did, that "if we give up our fundamental rights [of unfettered speech], the terrorists win."

But the umbrella of free speech was never intended to protect utterly offensive speech or comments that incite imminent harm, including murder or mass destruction.

## Abusing Free Speech Protection

And despite our open embrace of robust discussion and minimal intrusion on the parameters of open debate, there has never been sanctuary within the First Amendment for the expression of certain vile beliefs: Strident advocacy of child molestation or rape is not protected speech. The First Amendment does not protect words or actions of Nazis or the Ku Klux Klan or anyone explicitly advocating harm to an individual, especially on the basis of race or religion. It gives no safe harbor to those who would reveal secret U.S. Army plans in the midst of battle. It does not shield an elementary school teacher who utters obscenities in a classroom. And an entire body of law has grown around the notion of libel, the irresponsible utterances of untrue or hurtful comments about others, which lies outside the boundary of protected speech.

## Sick Violence Is Not Part of a Healthy Debate

Here is what YouTube said in response to Lieberman's letter:

> We believe that YouTube is a richer and more relevant platform for users precisely because it hosts

### There Have to Be Limits Online

Most of us recognise that there are limits on what we can say or do, limits imposed to benefit the wider society and which serve us all, even if they sometimes seem onerous. . . . Just as I can't expect to be allowed to wander into your home and shout at you because you spend your time watching trash TV instead of reading improving books, so my ability to say what I want on private forums is limited. The same principle applies to Slashdot, Digg, *The Guardian* or any other organization that hosts content.

Bill Thompson. "Which Freedoms Do We Want Online?" BBC.com, May 23, 2007. http://news.bbc.co.uk/2/hi/technology/6685253.stm.

a diverse range of views, and rather than stifle debate, we allow our users to view all acceptable content and make up their own minds. . . . Users are always free to express their disagreement . . . by leaving comments or their own response video. That debate is healthy.

Really? Would footage praising the slitting of the throat of American Daniel Pearl by terrorists be part of that "healthy" debate? Are propaganda films recruiting pre-teens to kill foreigners a "healthy" component on the debate on the Mideast? Are brutal acts of violence and degradation of women in music videos part of that "healthy" debate?

## We Are Confused About the Nature of Free Speech

As blogger Mark Hopkins noted in a recent post, YouTube seems confused. The site, in fact, does observe some standards of decency, but without any apparent consistency.

For instance, it yanked a video by a woman who created a montage of victims of terrorist attacks in the wake of the Mohammed cartoon controversy a few years back. YouTube said her montage promoted hate speech. But it permitted a video depicting homeless men pummeling each other after a filmmaker offered them sandwiches as pay.

It barred a video of a rap song with derogatory comments about women but gave a free pass to pornographic ads. It also barred a video of a woman breast-feeding a child and yanked footage captured by a witness to police brutality. If there is any logic to YouTube's sense of propriety, it escapes me.

YouTube's own policy stipulates it will not tolerate videos of "someone getting hurt, attacked or humiliated."

We can adhere to our principle of free and robust debate, but the *Times* should not fear that terrorists would "win" should reasonable restraints on abhorrent videos be made. The terrorists, however, may win if we befoul

our language by redefining healthy debate to include hosting video clips by religious fanatics embracing and encouraging mutilations, beheadings and assassinations of "infidels."

Lieberman is on target in his request for a consistent YouTube policy, and he should be praised for his efforts.

*Critics say that YouTube's policy of showing terrorist-sponsored videos is inconsistent.*

## Analyze the essay:

1. To make his argument that some material on the Internet should be censored, Peter Grad quotes from several sources. Make a list of everyone quoted, including their credentials and their relationship to his argument. In what way did these quotes enhance his argument?

2. Grad questions whether videos of beheadings and beatings qualify as constitutionally protected free speech. What do you think? Do such images have any merit that is worthy of being protected under the First Amendment? Explain your position on such material and whether you think it should be taken off the Internet.

# The Internet Should Not Be Censored

## Caroline Fredrickson

Caroline Fredrickson is the director of the Washington Legislative Office of the American Civil Liberties Union, a group whose mission is to protect the civil liberties of the American people, including their right under the First Amendment to free speech. In the following essay Fredrickson argues that the Internet should not be censored. First, she contends that the logistics of censoring the Internet are too difficult to overcome: Tech-savvy youth will be able to figure out how to get to censored material, and censoring something as vast and uncontrollable as the Internet would require a massive, expensive, and invasive government bureaucracy. Second, Fredrickson says that as the leading marketplace of ideas, the freedom of the Internet is valuable for promoting discussion, commerce, intellectual activity, and more. If the Internet is turned over to government or corporate censors who ban some material and push others, the unique nature of the Internet will be ruined. Fredrickson argues that the problem with censoring the Internet is the same as with censoring any medium: Once one piece of content is censored, all pieces of content are subject to censorship. Judging whether material is offensive enough to be censored is too subjective a job to give the government or censoring corporations, says Fredrickson, who warns that censors will soon ban anything they find objectionable, such as political expression and material that is in bad taste. Fredrickson concludes that more harm will be done by censoring Internet content than leaving it alone.

Caroline Fredrickson, *Testimony Before the House Committee on the Judiciary Task Force on Competition Policy and Antitrust Laws, Hearing on Net Neutrality and Free Speech on the Internet*. New York: American Civil Liberties Union, 2008. Reproduced by permission.

## Consider the following questions:

1. In what way is the Internet like a neutral "pipe," according to Fredrickson?
2. Who owns the Internet, in the author's opinion? Why is this special?
3. What was the finding of the 1996 Telecommunications Act, according to the author?

The Internet is one of today's most important means of disseminating information. "It enables people to communicate with one another with unprecedented speed and efficiency and is rapidly revolutionizing how people share and receive information."[1] It also provides "a forum for a true diversity of political discourse, unique opportunities for cultural development, and myriad avenues for intellectual activity."[2] These qualities make the Internet a shining example of a modern day marketplace of ideas.[3]

## The Leading Marketplace of Ideas

The Internet's marketplace enhances speech through its decentralized, neutral, nondiscriminatory "pipe" that automatically carries data from origin to destination without interference. Neutrality promotes open discourse. Consumers decide what sites to access, among millions of choices, and "pull" information from sites rather than having information chosen by others "pushed" out to them, as with television and other media in which the content is chosen by the broadcaster. The Internet's structure facilitates free speech, innovation, and competition on a global scale. Accessibility to a mass audience at little or no cost makes the Internet a particularly unique forum for speech. "The Internet presents low entry barriers to anyone who wishes to provide or distribute information. Unlike television, cable, radio, newspapers, magazines, or books, the Internet provides an opportunity for those with access to it to communicate with a worldwide audience at little cost."[4] "Any person with a phone line can become a town crier with a voice that resonates farther than it could from any soapbox."[5]

Furthermore, the Internet differs from other forms of mass communication because it "is really more idea than entity. It is an agreement we have made to hook our computers together and communicate by way of binary impulses and digitized signals."[6] No one "owns" the Internet. Instead, the Internet belongs to everyone

*Caroline Fredrickson, a director at the American Civil Liberties Union, testified before Congress about keeping the Internet uncensored.*

who uses it. The combination of these distinctive attributes allows the Internet to provide "a vast platform from which to address and hear from a worldwide audience of millions."[7]

Never before has it been so easy to circulate speech among so many people. John Doe can now communicate with millions of people from the comfort, safety and privacy of his own home. His communication requires minimal investment and minimal time—once the word is written, it is disseminated to a mass audience literally with the touch of a button. Moreover, Internet

## American Opinions of Internet Censorship

A 2006 study found that Americans are mixed on whether the Internet should publish content even if it is offensive, taboo, or dangerous.

*"I believe that certain information should not be published on the Internet."*

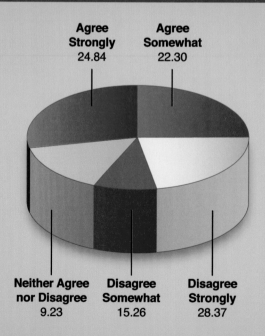

Agree Strongly 24.84

Agree Somewhat 22.30

Neither Agree nor Disagree 9.23

Disagree Somewhat 15.26

Disagree Strongly 28.37

Taken from: Craig A. Depken II, "Who Supports Internet Censorship?" *First Monday*, July 20, 2006. www.firstmonday.org/issues/issue11_9/depken/index.html#d3.

speakers are not restricted by the ordinary trappings of polite conversation; they tend to speak more freely online.[8]

"It is 'no exaggeration to conclude that the content on the Internet is as diverse as human thought.'"[9] "Such broad access to the public carries with it the potential to influence thought and opinion on a grand scale."[10] The Internet truly has become the leading 21st century marketplace of ideas because of neutrality rules that promote nondiscriminatory speech, association, and content.

## It Is Unrealistic to Censor the Web

**Automated censorship invariably ends up blocking much that it shouldn't. The results have been consistently absurd. . . . To block the huge amount of "explicit content" on thousands of servers all over the world would require a massive federal bureaucracy of censors and lawyers and prosecutors.**

Fred Reed, "Should Online Porn Be Barred?" *Washington Times*, January 5, 2008, p. C11.

## The Need to Protect Speech on the Internet

It is vital to the freedom of all Americans that free speech on the Internet be protected. Without question, the unique nature of the cyber revolution has posed some challenges in protecting the Internet.[11] Courts have confronted those challenges head on by observing, "Each medium of expression . . . may present its own problems."[12] Nevertheless, our "profound national commitment to the free exchange of ideas" requires that we meet those challenges to preserve Internet freedom.[13] We cannot sit idly by and let any censor stifle those freedoms, regardless of whether it is the government or a handful of network providers. In many communities, local governments have granted network providers monopolies to provide paying consumers with open Internet access. Widespread violations by ISPs [Internet service providers] highlight the need for congressional action to reinstate Internet nondiscrimination rules.

Courts acknowledge the importance of keeping the Web's channels of communication open and free from discrimination. The United States Supreme Court has concluded that speech on the Internet is entitled to the highest level of protection under the First Amendment. Any attempts to censor its content or silence its speakers are viewed with extreme disfavor.[14] In addition, courts recognize that the public has a First Amendment interest in receiving the speech and expression of others. "[T]he right of the public to receive suitable access to social, political, aesthetic, moral and other ideas and experiences" is one of the purposes served by the First Amendment.[15] Indeed, the "widest possible dissemination of information from diverse and antagonistic sources is essential to the welfare of the public."[16] The Internet has become the principal source for the public to access this diversity of ideas.[17]

## The Internet Belongs to Everyone

Courts also understand that "the Internet represents a brave new world of free speech."[18] Specifically, the Internet provides unique opportunities for speech and discourse. Unlike other media, *the Internet has no 'gate-keepers'—no publishers or editors controlling the distribution of information.*"[19] As a result, the Internet does not suffer from many of the limitations of alternative markets for the free exchange of ideas.[20] Therefore, courts have vigorously protected the public's right to uncensored Internet access on First Amendment grounds.[21]

In a similar vein, Congress has enacted legislation to protect and promote free speech on the Internet. In the 1996 Telecommunications Act, Congress found that "[t]he rapidly developing array of Internet and other interactive computer services available to individual Americans represent an extraordinary advance in the availability of educational and informational resources to our citizens."[22] Congress further declared that it is the policy of the United States "to encourage the development of technologies *which maximize user control over what information is received by individuals, families, and schools who use the Internet.*"[23] Congress therefore immunized Internet providers and users

from any liability for publishing "any information provided by another information content provider."[24]

## Information Must Flow Freely Online

Congressional creation and funding of federal agency web pages is further evidence of the need to facilitate the free flow of information on the Internet. In response to growing demand for online government resources, Congress enacted the E-Government Act of 2002 that

*Former President Bush signs the E-Government Act in December 2002 to improve the Internet's accessibility by the general public.*

created the Office of Electronic Government.[25] The Act's purpose "is to improve the methods by which Government information, including information on the Internet, is organized, preserved, and made accessible to the public."[26] Net neutrality advances that goal. As Congress has recognized on repeated occasions, it is in the public interest to promote the Internet's use as a forum to disseminate information and engage in free speech. . . .

## Keep the Internet Free

The growing prevalence of online censorship in the absence of neutrality rules no longer can be denied. Internet discrimination by ISPs is on the rise, and will only increase as more Americans rely upon the broadband services that they provide. I recommend in the strongest terms that the Task Force begin consideration of legislation that will protect the rights of all Internet users to send and receive content free of corporate censorship and provide meaningful remedies for violations. Otherwise, the Internet will be transformed from a shining oasis of speech to a desert of discrimination that serves to promote only the ISPs' commercial products.

## Notes

1. *Blumenthal v. Drudge*, 992 F. Supp. 44, 48 (D.D.C. 1998).

2. 47 U.S.C. § 230(a)(1)(3).

3. The "marketplace of ideas" is grounded in the belief that speech must be protected as a fundamental right for the discovery of truth. *See* JOHN STUART MILL, ON LIBERTY 76 (1859). Justice Oliver Wendell Holmes eloquently invoked the metaphor by observing, "when men have realized that time has upset many fighting faiths, they may come to believe even more than they believe the very foundations of their own conduct that the ultimate good desired is better reached by free trade in ideas—that the basic test of truth is

the power of the thought to get itself accepted in the competition of the market and that truth is the only ground upon which their wishes can be carried out." *Abrams v. United States*, 250 U.S. 616, 630 (1919) (Holmes, J., joined by Brandeis, J., dissenting). The marketplace of ideas metaphor aptly applies to an Internet free of corporate or government censors of lawful content. *See generally Reno v. ACLU*, 521 U.S. at 885 (rejecting government censorship of content in "the new marketplace of ideas," the Internet).

4. *American Library Ass'n v. United States*, 201 F. Supp.2d 401, 416 (E.D. Pa. 2002), *rev'd on other grounds*, 539 U.S. 194 (2003).

5. *Reno v. ACLU*, 521 U.S. at 870.

6. *Blumenthal*, 992 F. Supp. at 48 n.7 (quoting Brace W. Sanford & Michael J. Lorenger, *Teaching An Old Dog New Tricks; The First Amendment in an Online World*, 28 CONN. L. REV. 1137, 1139–43 (1996).

7. *Reno v. ACLU*, 521 U.S. at 853.

8. *Blumenthal*, 992 F. Supp. at 48 n.7 (quoting Sanford & Lorenger, *supra* note 6).

9. *Reno v. ACLU*, 521 U.S. at 852 (quoting *ACLU v. Reno*, 929 F. Supp. 824, 842 (E.D. Pa. 1996).

10. *Oja v. United States Army Corps of Eng'rs*, 440 F.3d 1122, 1129 (9th Cir. 2006).

11. *See Universal City Studios, Inc. v. Corley*, 273 F.3d 429, 433 (2d Cir. 2001).

12. *Southeastern Promotions Ltd. v. Conrad*, 420 U.S. 546, 557 (1975).

13. *Harte-Hanks Comm. Inc. v. Connaughton*, 491 U.S. 657, 686 (1989).

14. *See, e.g., Ashcroft v. ACLU*, 542 U.S. at 656 (upholding a preliminary injunction of the Child Online Protection Act); *Reno v. ACLU*, 521 U.S. at 844 (striking down certain provisions of the Communications Decency Act).

15. *Red Lion Broad. Co. v. FCC*, 395 U.S. 367, 390 (1969).

16. *Metro Broad. Inc. v. FCC*, 497 U.S. 547, 566–67 (1990) (quoting *Associated Press v. United States*, 326 U.S. 1, (1945).

17. Over one billion people have used the Internet, including nearly 70 percent of all people in North America. *See* http://www.internetworldstats.com/stats.htm (visited on Oct. 4, 2006).

18. *Blumenthal*, 992 F. Supp. at 48 n.7 (quoting Sanford & Lorenger, *supra* note 6).

19. *Id.* (emphasis added).

20. For example, under net neutrality, the Internet does not suffer from a criticism that Professor Laurence Tribe and other First Amendment scholars frequently have leveled at traditional marketplaces: "Especially when the wealthy have more access to the most potent media of communication than the poor, how sure can we be that 'free trade in ideas' is likely to generate truth?" LAURENCE H. TRIBE, AMERICAN CONSTITUTIONAL LAW 786 (2d ed. 1988).

21. *See supra* note 14 and accompanying text.

22. 47 U.S.C. § 230(a)(1).

23. 47 U.S.C. § 230(b)(3) (emphasis added).

24. 47 U.S.C. § 230(c)(1).

25. *See* Pub. L. No. 107–347, 116 Stat. 2899 (2002).

26. 44 U.S.C. § 3606 (a).

## Analyze the essay:

1. Fredrickson suggests that once Americans allow one type of message to be censored, nothing would stop other messages from being censored. What is your opinion of this argument? Does it convince you that nothing should be censored? Or, do you think it is possible to censor some material without threatening other material? Explain your answer using evidence from the texts you have read.

2. Fredrickson claims that keeping the Internet a free, open, and uncensored medium contributes to healthy, democratic intellectual debate. How do you think Peter Grad, author of the previous essay, would respond to this claim?

# Student Behavior Should Be Subject to Censorship

## Stanley Fish

In the following essay Stanley Fish argues that student behavior should be subject to censorship. He discusses a case in which a student, Joseph Frederick, was disciplined for carrying a drug-related banner during a school-sponsored event. Fish applauds the Supreme Court for deciding that Frederick's right to free speech had not been violated, because in Fish's opinion, students have no right to free speech while they are on school grounds. He argues that schools are institutions of teaching and learning, not of exploring and challenging. As such, a student's role is to absorb what is taught, not say anything and everything they want and have it unconditionally accepted. For these reasons, Fish concludes that student speech is not constitutionally protected and should be subject to censorship if it threatens the educational environment.

Fish is a professor of law at Florida International University and dean emeritus of the College of Liberal Arts

## Consider the following questions:

1. What was the outcome of the 1969 court case *Tinker v. Des Moines Independent Community School District*, as described by Fish?
2. What ten states does Fish say have ruled in some form or fashion that students do not have a right to free speech?
3. What does the word *pedagogy* mean in the context of the essay?

Stanley Fish, "Think Again: Clarence Thomas Is Right," *New York Times*, July 8, 2007. Reprinted with permission.

and Sciences at the University of Illinois at Chicago. He is the author of ten books, the most recent of which is *Save the World on Your Own Time*.

On June 25th the Supreme Court held in *Morse v. Frederick* that it was all right to discipline a high school student because he and some of his friends had unfurled a banner reading "Bong Hits 4 Jesus" at a school-sponsored event.

The facts are not in dispute. When the principal of the school, Deborah Morse, asked the students to take the banner down, one of them, Joseph Frederick, refused. He was suspended and his suspension was upheld by the school superintendent, who cited a board policy prohibiting any form of expression that "advocates the use of substances that are illegal to minors." Mr. Frederick then filed suit, alleging that his first amendment rights had been violated. A three-judge panel of the United States Court of Appeals for the Ninth Circuit agreed with him, but the Supreme Court reversed by a 5-to-4 vote, and held for Principal Morse.

The Court's discussion unfolds under the shadow of a 1969 case, *Tinker v. Des Moines Independent Community School District*, the key sentence of which declared that students do not "shed their constitutional rights to freedom of speech or expression at the schoolhouse gate." Not that students are free to say or express anything they like. The test, the Court said in *Tinker*, is whether the speech in question can be said to "materially and substantially disrupt the work and discipline of the school." In 1969, students had worn black armbands signifying their opposition to the Vietnam War. Applying the test it had just formulated, the Supreme Court held that since no such disruption was documented, the speech was protected.

The majority opinion in *Frederick*, written by Chief Justice John Roberts, ducks the disruption issue and

# Students and the First Amendment

Students say they do not care much about the First Amendment. In 2007 only a quarter of the nation's students personally think about the First Amendment, while 38 percent say they take it for granted.

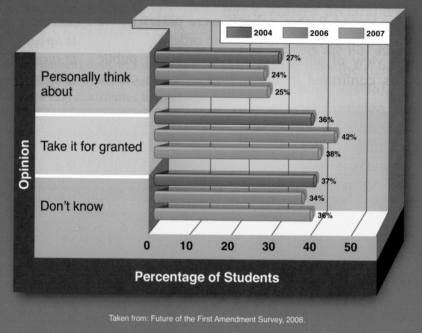

Taken from: Future of the First Amendment Survey, 2008.

in Vermont, Connecticut, Maine, Alabama, Tennessee, Kentucky, Indiana, North Carolina, California and Missouri, among others. It is only since *Tinker*—which, Thomas contends, "effected a sea change" in this area of law—that we have been troubled by talk of students' speech rights. (One suspects that Thomas is uneasy about the expansion of First Amendment rights in general. As recently as 1942, in *Chaplinsky v. New Hampshire*, the Court was able to rehearse a paragraph-long list of forms of speech that did not rise to the level of constitutional notice. That paragraph could not be written today.)

Although Thomas does not make this point explicitly, it seems clear that his approval of an older notion of the norms that govern student behavior stems from a conviction about how education should and should not proceed. When he tells us that it was traditionally understood that "teachers taught and students listened, teachers commanded and students obeyed," he comes across as someone who shares that understanding.

As do I. If I had a criticism of Thomas, it would be that he does not go far enough. Not only do students

*Supreme Court justice Clarence Thomas believes that the First Amendment to the Constitution does not afford the right of free speech in public schools.*

not have First Amendment rights, they do not have any rights: they don't have the right to express themselves, or have their opinions considered, or have a voice in the evaluation of their teachers, or have their views of what should happen in the classroom taken into account. (And I intend this as a statement about college students as well as high-school students.)

One reason that students (and many others) have come to believe that they have these rights is a confusion between education and democracy. It is in democratic contexts that people have claims to the rights enumerated in the constitution and other documents at the heart of our political system—the right to free speech, the right to free assembly, the right to determine, by vote, the shape of their futures.

Educational institutions, however, are not democratic contexts (even when the principles of democracy are being taught in them). They are pedagogical contexts and the imperatives that rule them are the imperatives of pedagogy—the mastery of materials and the acquiring of analytical skills. Those imperatives do not recognize the right of free expression or any other right, except the right to competent instruction, that is, the right to be instructed by well-trained, responsible teachers who know their subjects and stick to them and don't believe that it is their right to pronounce on anything and everything.

What this means is that teachers don't have First Amendment rights either, at least while they are performing as teachers. Away from school, they have the same rights as anyone else. In school, they are just like their students, bound to the protocols of the enterprise they have joined. That enterprise is not named democracy and what goes on within it—unless it is abuse or harassment or assault—should not rise to the level of constitutional notice or any other notice except the notice of the professional authorities whose job it is to keep the educational machine running smoothly.

## Analyze the essay:

1. Stanley Fish used Supreme Court case outcomes to provide evidence for his argument. Did these pieces of evidence help persuade you to agree with him? Why or why not?

2. Fish argues that because students in public schools are there to learn what is taught to them, they are not democratic places where free speech is protected. Do you agree with this understanding of the nature of school? Explain your answer using evidence from the text.

# Student Behavior Should Not Be Subject to Censorship

Bruce Fein

In the following essay Bruce Fein argues that student behavior should not be subject to censorship. He discusses the case of Tyler Harper, a Poway, California, high school student who wore antigay T-shirts to school. The Supreme Court ruled that Harper did not have a right to wear such shirts because they impinged upon the rights of gay students at his school. Fein, however, disagrees. He says that Harper was merely expressing his beliefs in a calm, controlled, nonviolent way. In his opinion, Harper has as much a right to voice his opinion of homosexuals as homosexuals have to voice their opinion of him. He also says that schools are nothing if not a place where students are taught they have the right to form and express opinions. Though Harper's beliefs may not be popular, Fein concludes they should still be constitutionally protected.

Fein is a constitutional lawyer and international consultant with Bruce Fein and Associates and the Lichfield Group.

## Consider the following questions:

1. What is high school dress rehearsal for, according to Fein?
2. What slogans appeared on Tyler Harper's T-shirts, as reported by the author?
3. Where do at least 90 percent of our beliefs come from, in Fein's opinion?

Justice Oliver Wendell Holmes explained the folly of public school speech codes that seek to shield students from anguishing ideas or assertions in *United States v. Schwimmer* (1929):

"[I]f there is any principle of the Constitution that more importantly calls for the attachment than any other it is the principle of free thought—not free thought for those that agree with us but freedom for the thought that we hate." Yet the U.S. 9th Circuit Court of Appeals sustained a school code that prohibited T-shirts disparaging homosexuality in *Harper v. Poway United School District* (April 20).

*What students can say about sexual orientation on school grounds is one of the many free speech issues that have been considered by the Supreme Court.*

High school should be a dress rehearsal for political participation and debate where disagreeable or vituperative views are regularly encountered. The franchise is constitutionally conferred at 18. The Harper precedent is thus appalling.

Sexual orientation has provoked controversy at Poway High School and sister schools nationally for several years. The student exchanges are the minor leagues of the sparring in Congress, state legislatures, and city

## Censorship of High School Publications

Recent cases of censorship of high school publications include:

| High School | Location | Publication | Issue |
|---|---|---|---|
| Woodlan High School | East Allen County, IN | *The Tomahawk* | tolerance of homosexuality |
| Benson High School | Omaha, NE | *Benson Gazette* | racist language |
| Olentangy Liberty High School | Powell, OH | *Cannon* | sexual content |
| Olentangy High School | Lewis Center, OH | *Beacon* | sexual content |
| Vashon High School | Vashon, WA | *The Riptide* | criticism of school official |
| Danbury High School | Danbury, TX | *Panther Press* | sexually-themed stories |
| St. Francis High School | St. Francis, MN | *The Crier* | image of torn U.S. flag |
| Lake Stevens High School | Lake Stevens, WA | *Valhalla* | controversial class/ personal information about a faculty member |
| Princeton High School | Cincinnati, OH | *Odin's World* | criticism of school football team |
| Flint Kearsley High School | Flint, MI | *The Eclipse* | ongoing censorship |
| Chelsea High School | Chelsea, MI | *Bleu Print* | ongoing censorship |
| Belleville High School East | Belleville, IL | *Terrace Scroll* | principal editing papers |
| Winnacunnet High School | Winnacunnet, NH | *Winnachronicle* | sexual stories |

councils over same-sex "marriage," homosexual parenting, legal protections against discrimination, and "don't ask, don't tell" in the military. In 2003, a student group called the Gay-Straight Alliance at Poway held a "Day of Silence" protesting denigration of homosexuals. Student opponents responded with T-shirts derogatory of gays and lesbians.

During the April 21, 2004, "Day of Silence" to challenge student endorsement or acceptance of homosexuality,

| High School | Location | Publication | Issue |
|---|---|---|---|
| Montrose High School | Montrose, PA | *Meteor Chronicle* | teenage sexuality |
| East Jordan High School | East Jordan, MI | *The Devil's Advocate* | ongoing censorship |
| East Grand Forks Senior High School | East Grand Forks, MN | *Green Crest* | ongoing censorship |
| Southeast High School | Los Angeles, CA | *Jaguar Times* | random searches on campus |
| Wyoming Valley West High School | Plymouth, PA | *Interim, Literary Arts Magazine* | poem about a teacher catching a student without a hall pass |
| Claremont High School | Claremont, CA | *The Wolfpacket* | permanent substitute hiring |
| Burleson High School | Burleson, TX | *Newsrack* | ongoing censorship |
| Truman High School | Independence, MO | *The Spirit* | student drug use |
| East Bakersfield High School | East Bakersfield, CA | *The Kernal* | teen homosexuality |
| Everett High School | Everett, WA | *Kodak* | ongoing censorship and subsequent lawsuit |
| Carson High School | Carson, CA | *Trailblazer* | legalization of marijuana; masturbation and sexual freedom |
| Deltona High School | Deltona, FL | *Paw Print* | criticism of school spending |
| Hillsborough High School | Tampa, FL | *Red & Black* | achievement gap between students |
| Ramapo High School | Franklin Lakes, NJ | *Rampage* | student drug use |

Taken from: Wendy Wallace, and Audrey Wagstaff, Scholastic Journalism Center at Kent State University, 2007.

Tyler Chase Harper wore a T-shirt with two handwritten declarations: "I will not accept what God has condemned," and, "Homosexuality is shameful 'Romans 1:27.'" Nothing untoward ensued. The following day, the T-shirt was again worn, but with the former message altered to read "Be ashamed, our school embraced what God condemned."

Tyler Harper neither stalked putative homosexuals nor flaunted his T-shirt with the intent of inciting illegal conduct. No classroom fell into acrimony. No altercation erupted. His second-period teacher observed several students talking about the shirt "off-task." But instead of admonishing the students' misbehavior, the teacher cited Tyler for a dress code violation. The assistant principal and principal sought to persuade him to remove the T-shirt because [it was] inflammatory or mean-spirited. He persisted. He remained in the front office until the end of the school day, and was told he could not wear the T-shirt on campus.

Tyler Harper initiated litigation arguing censorship of speech condemnatory of homosexuality violated the First Amendment's protection of free speech. The court of appeals denied the claim. It insisted gay and lesbian students are psychologically traumatized by words or symbols that might make them feel inferior. Their educational development is stunted. Thus, schools are endowed with a compelling interest in shielding students from ideas or assertions they despise or find unsettling. Speaking for a 2-1 panel majority, Judge Stephen Reinhardt amplified: "Those who administer our public educational institutions need not tolerate verbal assaults that may destroy the self-esteem of our most vulnerable teenagers and interfere with their educational development."

But the whole purpose of the First Amendment, as Justice Holmes underscored in *Schwimmer*, is the opposite. Other than idle social chatter, speech that fails to arouse opposition from someone is probably not worth saying.

*Supreme Court Justice Oliver Wendell Holmes argued in* **United States v. Schwimmer** *that the First Amendment protects all forms of speech, even unpopular ones.*

Freedom of speech protects hated or reviled expression because prevailing orthodoxies may be wrong.

Time has upset many fighting faiths. Under the crabbed conception of the First Amendment embraced in *Harper*, however, 19th century public school authorities could have banned students from touting William Lloyd Garrison, Elizabeth Cady Stanton, or Charles Darwin because some of their classmates might have been emotionally distraught over speech that denounced

## Students Have the Same Constitutional Right to Free Speech as Others

If college students have no more Constitutional protections than first graders do, then college professors may have no more rights than elementary school teachers. . . . If "academic freedom" means only the power of administrators to "manage an academic community," then students and professors alike will be subject to censorship by the administration.

John K. Wilson, "The Case of the Censored Newspaper," *Inside Higher Ed*, June 24, 2005. www.insidehighered.com/views/2005/06/24/wilson.

slavery, promoted women's rights, or endorsed the theory of man's evolution from a lower order of species.

A school's proper educational mission is to expose students to a cornucopia of ideas and viewpoints to enable independent judgment and sturdy convictions that motivate action. Ninety percent or more of what we believe comes from knowing why alternative claims are unconvincing. If antagonistic theories are not encountered, beliefs become shallow and ritualistic rather than deep and abiding. They will neither be robustly defended nor stir to action.

The *Harper* precedent makes the pope's ill-conceived index of forbidden books seem liberal in comparison. All student speech can be suppressed so the self-esteem of all may remain unchallenged. T-shirts characterizing the Irish potato famine as genocide may be banned because students of British background may be psychologically disquieted. Expression condemning the invasion and occupation of Iraq by the United States may be prohibited to protect the sensitivities of students whose parents have died in the fighting. Indeed, T-shirts reading, "Opposition to homosexuality is shameful," might be enjoined because they are held deflating to opponents' self-esteem.

*Harper* is not defensible on the theory that students are a captive audience. They can as easily avert their eyes from obnoxious T-shirts as motorists passing drive-in movie theaters can avert their eyes from nudity or violence. As to the latter, the Supreme Court elaborated in *Erzoznik v. City of Jacksonville* (1975) that the minor irritant to the viewer is a small price to pay for preserving the First Amendment.

## Analyze the essay:

1. Bruce Fein, the author of this essay, and Stanley Fish, the author of the previous essay, are both lawyers. However, they come to very different conclusions about whether student behavior should be subject to censorship. How might you explain this discrepancy given the fact that they have the same profession?

2. Bruce Fein argues that students should be allowed to wear antigay T-shirts in school because of their right to free speech. If someone at your school wore T-shirts with slogans that maligned a certain group of people, or even your race, religion, or sexual orientation, how would you feel? Would you support that person's right to wear such a shirt? Explain your reasoning.

# Section Two: Model Essays and Writing Exercises

# The Five-Paragraph Essay

An *essay* is a short piece of writing that discusses or analyzes one topic. The five-paragraph essay is a form commonly used in school assignments and tests. Every five-paragraph essay begins with an *introduction*, ends with a *conclusion*, and features three *supporting paragraphs* in the middle.

**The Thesis Statement.** The introduction includes the essay's thesis statement. The thesis statement presents the argument or point the author is trying to make about the topic. The essays in this book all have different thesis statements because they are making different arguments about censorship.

The thesis statement should clearly tell the reader what the essay will be about. A focused thesis statement helps determine what will be in the essay; the subsequent paragraphs are spent developing and supporting its argument.

**The Introduction.** In addition to presenting the thesis statement, a well-written introductory paragraph captures the attention of the reader and explains why the topic being explored is important. It may provide the reader with background information on the subject matter or feature an anecdote that illustrates a point relevant to the topic. It could also present startling information that clarifies the point of the essay or put forth a contradictory position that the essay will refute. Further techniques for writing an introduction are found later in this section.

**The Supporting Paragraphs.** The introduction is followed by three (or more) supporting paragraphs. These are the main body of the essay. Each paragraph presents and develops a *subtopic* that supports the essay's thesis statement. Each subtopic is spearheaded by a *topic sentence* and supported by its own facts, details, and examples. The writer can use various kinds of supporting material and details to back up the topic of each supporting paragraph. These may include statistics, quotations from people with special knowledge or expertise, historic facts, and anecdotes. A rule of writing is that specific and concrete examples are more convincing than vague, general, or unsupported assertions.

*The Conclusion.* The conclusion is the paragraph that closes the essay. Its function is to summarize or reiterate the main idea of the essay. It may recall an idea from the introduction or briefly examine the larger implications of the thesis. Because the conclusion is also the last chance a writer has to make an impression on the reader, it is important that it not simply repeat what has been presented elsewhere in the essay but close it in a clear, final, and memorable way.

Although the order of the essay's component paragraphs is important, they do not have to be written in the order presented here. Some writers like to decide on a thesis and write the introduction paragraph first. Other writers like to focus first on the body of the essay and write the introduction and conclusion later.

## Pitfalls to Avoid

When writing essays about controversial issues such as censorship, it is important to remember that disputes over the material are common precisely because there are many different perspectives. Remember to state your arguments in careful and measured terms. Evaluate your topic fairly—avoid overstating negative qualities of one perspective or understating positive qualities of another. Use examples, facts, and details to support any assertions you make.

# The Expository Essay

The previous section of this book provided you with samples of writings on censorship. All made arguments or advocated a particular position about free speech, the First Amendment, censorship, and related topics. All included elements of *expository* writing as well. The purpose of expository writing is to inform the reader about a particular subject. Sometimes a writer will use exposition to simply communicate knowledge; other times, he or she will use exposition to persuade a reader of a particular point of view.

## Types of Expository Writing

There are several different types of expository writing. Examples of these types can be found in the viewpoints in the preceding chapter. The list below provides some ideas on how exposition could be organized and presented. Each type of writing could be used separately or in combination in five-paragraph essays.

*Definition.* Definition refers to simply telling what something is. Definitions can be encompassed in a sentence or paragraph. At other times, definitions may take a paragraph or more. The act of defining some topics—especially abstract concepts—can sometimes serve as the focus of entire essays. An example of definition is found in Viewpoint Two by the American Press Institute. The authors of that piece attempt to define "terrorist speech" to show that it is nearly impossible to do so without including other kinds of speech that, even if unpopular, is constitutionally protected.

*Classification.* A classification essay describes and clarifies relationships between things by placing them in different categories based on their similarities and differences. This can be a good way of organizing and

67

presenting information. Viewpoint Three by Peter Grad uses classification—the author classifies certain forms of expression (such as open debate and political disagreement) as being constitutionally protected forms of free speech and classifies other forms of expression (such as those that incite murder, rape, or child molestation) as sick violence that are not protected.

*Process.* A process essay looks at how something is done. The writer presents events or steps in a chronological or ordered sequence of steps. Process writing can either inform the reader of a past event or process by which something was made, or instruct the reader on how to do something.

*Illustration.* Illustration is one of the simplest and most common patterns of expository writing. Simply put, it explains by giving specific and concrete examples. It is an effective technique for making one's writing both more interesting and more intelligible. An example of illustration is found in Viewpoint One by Newt Gingrich. He uses illustration when he tells the story of the "flying Imams" to make his point that Americans must not allow terrorists to hide behind the First Amendment.

## Words and Phrases Common to Expository Essays

Writers use these words and phrases to explain their subjects, to provide transitions between paragraphs, and to summarize key ideas in an essay's concluding paragraph.

| | |
|---|---|
| accordingly | indeed |
| because | it is important to understand |
| clearly | it makes sense to |
| consequently | it seems as though |
| evidently | it then follows that |
| first . . . second . . . third . . . | moreover |
| for example | since |
| for this reason | subsequently |
| from this perspective | therefore |
| furthermore | this is why |
| however | thus |

***Problem/solution.*** Problem/solution refers to when the author raises a problem or a question and then uses the rest of the paragraph or essay to answer the question or provide possible resolutions to the problem. It can be an effective way of drawing in the reader while imparting information to him/her.

# Not All Speech Is Free Speech

**Editor's Notes** The following five-paragraph essay uses classification as an organizing principle. A classification essay describes and clarifies relationships between things by placing them in different categories. You can read more about classification essays (and other types of expository essays) in Preface B of this section.

The following essay classifies certain forms of expression (such as open debate and political disagreement) as constitutionally protected forms of free speech and classifies other forms of expression (such as the speech of terrorists) as speech that is not protected. The notes in the margin point out key features of the essay and help you understand how it is organized. Also note that all sources are cited using Modern Language Association (MLA) style.* For more information on how to cite your sources, see Appendix C. In addition, consider the following:

1. How does the introduction engage the reader's attention?
2. What pieces of supporting evidence are used to back up the essay's points and arguments?
3. What purpose do the essay's quotes serve?
4. How does the author transition from one idea to another?
5. How is classification featured in the essay?

*Editor's Note: In applying MLA style guidelines in this book, the following simplifications have been made: Parenthetical text citations are confined to direct quotations only; electronic source documentation in the Works Cited list omits date of access, page ranges, and some detailed facts of publication.

## Paragraph 1

In a world where guns, bombs, and explosions grab a lot of attention, we sometimes forget about the power of words. But words can make us want to laugh and cry, and they make us feel angry, remorseful, or bittersweet. America's founding fathers understood the power of words, which is why they enshrined the freedom of speech into the Bill of Rights. But not all speech qualifies as free speech, and it is important to make distinctions between protected and unprotected forms of speech so that our Constitution does not protect the words of people who aim to harm or degrade our society.

This is the essay's thesis statement. It gets to the heart of the author's argument.

## Paragraph 2

The First Amendment should always protect contentious, critical, and even unpopular speech. Examples of speech that is constitutionally protected include that which contributes to healthy political or social debate, criticisms of social or moral policy, unbridled criticism of government and religious leaders, and even explicit or indecent material online (as the Supreme Court unanimously ruled in the 1997 case *Reno v. American Civil Liberties Union*). These are all examples of speech that is in the spirit of what the authors of the First Amendment meant when they wrote "Congress shall make no law . . . abridging the freedom of speech."

This is the topic sentence of Paragraph 2. Note that all of the paragraph's details fit with it—or *support* it.

## Paragraph 3

Yet the First Amendment was not intended to be a security blanket for *any* form of speech, a point on which many Americans appear confused. Merely saying *something* is not grounds for it to be protected. "The umbrella of free speech was never intended to protect utterly offensive speech or comments that incite imminent harm, including murder or mass destruction," explains columnist Peter Grad. "There has never been sanctuary within the First Amendment for the expression of certain vile beliefs." (F8) Terrorist speech, along

What is the topic sentence of Paragraph 3? Look for a sentence that tells generally what the paragraph's main point is.

This quote was taken from Viewpoint Three of this book. Use strong, interesting, and relevant quotes to support points you make in your essays.

with the words and ideas of child pornographers, rapists, murderers, and others, should never be—and are not—shielded by the Constitution. It is important to remember that this document offers American citizens their most precious and cherished rights—to use it as a shield to protect the most vile members of society disrespects this cherished document and the founders who wrote it.

What features of this essay let you know it is making classifications?

### Paragraph 4

How can we determine what speech falls within the boundaries of protected speech and what does not? A simple principle by former House Speaker Newt Gingrich offers a clear, guiding line: "Free speech should not be an acceptable cover for people who are planning to kill other people." Using this as a guiding rule, Web sites that feature terrorist rants about how Americans should be killed should be immediately taken down, as should videos that show the grisly murder of innocents abroad (such as the beheading of Daniel Pearl or Nicholas Berg, whose murders were filmed by Iraqi terrorists and pasted all over the Internet). While this rule does not go far enough to cover the expression of child molesters (whose speech should never be protected), it is a good starting point for differentiating between acceptable and unacceptable forms of free speech.

Identify a piece of evidence used to support Paragraph 4's main idea.

### Paragraph 5

Words are as powerful as the strength we give them. When we protect the words of terrorists under the banner of speech, we legitimize the ideas they espouse. We should not allow our Constitution to be used against us in this way. All Americans must work to honor the true meaning of the First Amendment by not granting all speech the protection of free speech.

Note how the author returns to ideas introduced in Paragraph 1. See Exercise 2B for more on introductions and conclusions.

# Works Cited

Gingrich, Newt. "The 1st Amendment Is Not a Suicide Pact: Blocking the Speech That Calls for Our Death." *Human Events* 4 Dec. 2006 < http://www.humanevents. com/article.php?id = 18314 > .

Grad, Peter. "Terrorists' Videos Don't Belong on YouTube." *Record* [Bergen County, NJ] 31 May 2008: F8.

## Exercise 1A: Create an Outline from an Existing Essay

It often helps to create an outline of the five-paragraph essay before you write it. The outline can help you organize the information, arguments, and evidence you have gathered during your research.

For this exercise, create an outline that could have been used to write "Not All Speech Is Free Speech." This "reverse engineering" exercise is meant to help familiarize you with how outlines can help classify and arrange information.

To do this you will need to
1. articulate the essay's thesis,
2. pinpoint important pieces of evidence,
3. flag quotes that supported the essay's ideas, and
4. identify key points that supported the argument.

Part of the outline has already been started to give you an idea of the assignment.

## Outline

**I. Paragraph 1**

**Write the essay's thesis or main objective:** Not all speech qualifies as free speech.

**II. Paragraph 2**
**Topic:**

> **Supporting Detail i.** Speech that criticizes government leaders is an example of speech that is constitutionally protected.

> **Supporting Detail ii.**

## III. Paragraph 3
**Topic:**

    **Supporting Detail i.** Quote by Peter Grad about what kinds of speech are not protected by the First Amendment.

    **Supporting Detail ii.**

## IV. Paragraph 4
**Topic:** Speech that espouses the murder of innocents is a good place to draw the line at what counts and doesn't count as free speech.

    **Supporting Detail i.**

    **Supporting Detail ii.**

## V. Paragraph 5
**Write the essay's conclusion:**

## Exercise 1B: Create an Outline for Your Own Essay

The first model essay expresses a particular point of view about censorship and free speech. For this exercise, your assignment is to find supporting ideas, choose specific and concrete details, create an outline, and ultimately write a five-paragraph essay making a different, even opposing, point about free speech. Your goal is to use narrative techniques to convince your reader.

## Part I: Write a thesis statement.

The following thesis statement would be appropriate for an opposing expository essay on why it is dangerous to classify some forms of speech as unworthy of protection:

> *Once you start drawing the line between what counts as free speech and what counts as illegal speech, the entire concept of freedom of expression becomes jeopardized.*

Or, see the sample paper topics suggested in Appendix D for more ideas.

## Part II: Brainstorm pieces of supporting evidence.

Using information found in this book and from your own research, write down three arguments or pieces of evidence that support the thesis statement you selected. Then, for each of these three arguments, write down facts, examples, and details that support it. These could be

- statistical information;
- personal memories and anecdotes;
- quotes from experts, peers, or family members;
- observations of people's actions and behaviors;
- specific and concrete details.

Supporting pieces of evidence for the above sample thesis statement might include:

- The quote in Viewpoint Two by the American Press Institute that banning hate or terrorist speech does not eliminate hate or terrorism—it merely eliminates freedom for everyone: "Banning speech about hate, after all, does not eliminate hate or violence. But it may eliminate a fundamental freedom—and illuminate the fragility of Americans' attachment to all other freedoms."
- The point made in Viewpoint Two about the slippery slope that emerges when one seeks to classify *some* speech as censorable: You cannot censor one type of speech without subjecting all of it to censorship.
- The point made in Viewpoint Four by Caroline Fredrickson about the political, social, and economic benefits of an unfiltered, uncensored Internet—even if that means living with an Internet that is home to indecent, unpopular, or even violent postings.

## Part III: Place the information from Part I in outline form.

## Part IV: Write the arguments or supporting statements in paragraph form.

By now you have three arguments that support the essay's thesis statement, as well as supporting material. Use the outline to write out your three supporting arguments in paragraph form. Make sure each paragraph has a topic sentence that states the paragraph's thesis clearly and broadly. Then, add sentences that express the facts, quotes, details, and examples that support the paragraph's argument. The paragraph may also have a concluding or summary sentence.

# Why Censorship Is Not the Solution for the Web

**Editor's Notes** One way of writing an expository essay is to use the "problem/solution" method. Problem/solution refers to when the author raises a problem or a question and then uses the rest of the paragraph or essay to answer the question or provide solutions to the problem.

The second model essay uses a twist on the problem/solution method to argue that the Internet should not be censored. The author offers three reasons why censoring the Internet will not sufficiently solve the problem of objectionable online content.

Like the first model essay, this essay uses expository writing techniques to convince the reader of a particular argument—this makes it a *persuasive* essay in addition to an *expository* essay. Rather than merely explaining an issue, idea, or event, it attempts to convince the reader of a particular point of view. While exposition is a good medium for neutral or informational essays, it can also work for essays in which the author wants to argue a point.

As you did with the first essay, use the notes in the margins to figure out how this essay is organized and written.

■ Refers to thesis and topic sentences

■ Refers to supporting details

**Paragraph 1**

The author opens the essay by establishing a problem—the presence of offensive content on the Internet. The solution, however, is not to censor the Internet. The rest of the essay will focus on explaining why.

The Internet is like no other medium in human history. Perhaps a three-judge panel, ruling in the case *ACLU v. Reno*, put it best when it stated, "It is no exaggeration to conclude that the content on the Internet is as diverse as human thought." Indeed, the Internet reflects the totality of the human experience—and this means it features the good, the bad, the ugly; the perverse, the beautiful, the mundane. That humans are such diverse creatures is at times problematic, such as when we use our creativity for seedy purposes, or when we use our voices to inspire hatred against others. But while the Internet is home to much content that does not contribute positively to society, the solution is not to censor it. Censoring the Internet is the wrong approach to solving the age-old problem of dealing with offensive or objectionable content.

### Paragraph 2

To grasp the futility of trying to censor the Internet, start by imagining the logistics of such a project. As of 2007, the group Netcraft, a widely respected Internet survey company, estimated the number of Web sites at more than 108 million—many of which have thousands of subpages. But no one really knows for sure, since no central body governs the Internet. In addition to being mammoth, the Internet is a constantly changing, growing, almost living medium that does not keep still long enough to censor. For this reason columnist Fred Reed has said, "To block the huge amount of 'explicit content' on thousands of servers all over the world would require a massive federal bureaucracy of censors and lawyers and prosecutors." (C11) In addition to being complicated and overbearing, such a bureaucracy would be unreasonably expensive: In 2007 Australia's government proposed an Internet censoring program that would cost $84.4 million dollars. And, in the end, tech-savvy people would probably find their way around censorship walls anyway—this was the case when an Australian teenager hacked the new censorship software almost immediately after its development.

### Paragraph 3

Second, censoring the Internet requires putting people in charge of determining what material is objectionable and what is not—a sensitive process that too often blurs the line between offensive and unpopular. Indeed, the problem with censoring the Internet is the same as

This is the essay's thesis statement. It gets to the heart of the author's argument.

This fact helps support one of the paragraph's main ideas: that the Internet is too large to censor. Get in the habit of supporting the points you make with facts, quotes, statistics, and anecdotes.

This quote was taken from the quote box that accompanies Viewpoint Four. When you see striking quotes, save them to use in your essays.

This is the topic sentence of Paragraph 3. Without reading the rest of the paragraph, take a guess at what the paragraph will be about.

with censoring any medium: Once one piece of content is censored, all pieces of content are subject to censorship. But judging whether material is offensive enough to be censored is too subjective a job to hire government or corporate employees to do. Perhaps most people could agree that a video of two people having intercourse constitutes pornography, but what about a nude painting by a famous artist? Should that be banned from the Internet—despite the fact that such images are featured in art history courses around the country? The slippery slope that emerges when one seeks to classify censorable material is evidence that you cannot censor one type of material without subjecting all of it to censorship.

### Paragraph 4

What is the topic sentence of Paragraph 4? Look for a sentence that tells generally what the paragraph's main point is.

Third, the Internet is the world's most valuable forum for communication and even democracy, and as such, it is too important to tamper with. The Internet has become the leading medium for political ideas and debate, especially in countries famous for political repression, such as Burma, Iran, and China. In these places free speech is so limited that people must go online to have the kinds of discussions they would have out in the open in other nations. As a result, blocking, editing, or censoring any portion of the Internet can have grave consequences for political freedom all over the world. This is why technology commentator Seth Finkelstein has warned that censoring the Internet would threaten burgeoning democratic movements around the world. As Finkelstein has put it, "If you block online porn, you'll surely block dissent in China." (2)

"As a result" is a transitional phrase. It links the author's sentences and keeps her ideas moving forward.

### Paragraph 5

Rather than wasting time, spending valuable resources, and squandering cherished values attempting to censor the Internet, a better response to inappropriate online content is to approach it in the same way "bad" speech has been dealt with throughout much of American history: by countering it with words that expose its logical and moral bankruptcy. Rather than outlawing objectionable speech, let us answer it with ideas that are more attractive. "Banning speech about hate, after all, does not eliminate hate or violence," explains the American Press Institute. But it does threaten a cherished freedom—one none of us can afford to lose.

> The author concludes by suggesting an alternative to censorship. Strive to end your essays by offering solutions, calls to action, or other productive ideas that the reader can consider.

## Works Cited

*ACLU v. Reno.* 929 F. Supp. 824, 842 (E.D. Pa. 1996).

Finkelstein, Seth. "Technology: Read Me First: If You Block Online Porn, You'll Surely Block Dissent in China." *Guardian* [London] 17 Apr. 2008: 2.

Reed, Fred. "Should Online Porn Be Barred?" *Washington Times* 5 Jan. 2008: C11.

## Exercise 2A: Create an Outline from an Existing Essay

As you did for the first model essay in this section, create an outline that could have been used to write "Why Censorship Is Not the Solution for the Web." Be sure to identify the essay's thesis statement, its supporting ideas, and key pieces of evidence that were used.

## Exercise 2B: Examining Introductions and Conclusions

Whether an essay is a first-person account, a report on an event, or a formal persuasive paper, all pieces of writing feature introductory and concluding paragraphs that are used to frame the main ideas being presented. Along with presenting the essay's thesis statement, well-written introductions should grab the attention of the reader and make clear why the topic being explored is important. The conclusion reiterates the essay's thesis and is also the last chance for the writer to make an impression on the reader. Strong introductions and conclusions can greatly enhance an essay's effect on an audience.

### The Introduction

Several techniques can be used to craft an introductory paragraph. An essay can start with:

- an anecdote: a brief story that illustrates a point relevant to the topic;
- startling information: facts or statistics that elucidate the point of the essay;
- setting up and knocking down a position: a position or claim believed by proponents of one side of a controversy, followed by statements that challenge that claim;
- historical perspective: an example of the way things used to be that leads into a discussion of how or why things work differently now;

- summary information: general introductory information about the topic that feeds into the essay's thesis statement.

1. Reread the introductory paragraphs of the model essays and of the viewpoints in Section One. Identify which of the techniques described above are used in the example essays. How do they grab the attention of the reader? Are their thesis statements clearly presented?

2. Write an introduction for the essay you have outlined and partially written in Exercise 1B using one of the techniques described above.

## The Conclusion

The conclusion brings the essay to a close by summarizing or returning to its main ideas. Good conclusions, however, go beyond simply repeating these ideas. Strong conclusions explore a topic's broader implications and reiterate why it is important to consider. They may frame the essay by returning to an anecdote featured in the opening paragraph. Or they may close with a quotation or refer to an event in the essay. In opinionated essays, the conclusion can reiterate which side the essay is taking or ask the reader to reconsider a previously held position on the subject.

3. Reread the concluding paragraphs of the model essays and of the viewpoints in Section One. Which were most effective in driving home their arguments to the reader? What sorts of techniques did they use to do this? Did they appeal emotionally to the reader, or bookend an idea or event referenced elsewhere in the essay?

4. Write a conclusion for the essay you have outlined and partially written in Exercise 1B using one of the techniques described above.

## Exercise 2C: Using Quotations to Enliven Your Essay

No essay is complete without quotations. Get in the habit of using quotes to support at least some of the ideas in your essays. Quotes do not need to appear in every paragraph, but often enough so that the essay contains voices aside from your own. When you write, use quotations to accomplish the following:

- Provide expert advice that you are not necessarily in the position to know about.
- Cite lively or passionate passages.
- Include a particularly well-written point that gets to the heart of the matter.
- Supply statistics or facts that have been derived from someone's research.
- Deliver anecdotes that illustrate the point you are trying to make.
- Express first-person testimony.

*Problem One*
Reread the essays presented in all sections of this book and find at least one example of each of the above quotation types.

There are a couple of important things to remember when using quotations:

- Note your sources' qualifications and biases. This way your reader can identify the person you have quoted and can put their words in a context.
- Put any quoted material within proper quotation marks. Failing to attribute quotes to their authors constitutes plagiarism, which is when an author takes someone else's words or ideas and presents them as his or her own. Plagiarism is a very serious infraction and must be avoided at all costs.

# When Student Newspapers Are Censored: One School's Story

**Editor's Notes** The third model essay discusses censorship using a different aspect of the expository essay. It reports on the censorship of a student publication. Reporting on an event is a common expository technique used every day in newspapers, magazines, and journals. Unlike the previous model essays, this essay does not attempt to persuade you of a point of view or opinion—it simply presents the information and lets you draw your own conclusion on the matter.

To write this essay, the author conducted interviews with students and school administrators. The information gleaned during the course of the interviews allowed the author to get inside information, details, and opinions on the event. Because they yield these types of details, interviews can be a useful tool when writing an expository essay. More information about conducting an interview is found in Exercises 3A and 3B that follow the essay.

Also, unlike the previous essays, the following essay is longer than five paragraphs. Sometimes five paragraphs are simply not enough to adequately develop an idea. Extending the length of an essay can allow the reader to explore a topic in more depth. Longer essays also help readers discover the complexity of a subject by examining a topic beyond its superficial exterior. The ability to write a sustained research or position paper is a valuable skill you will need as you advance academically.

■ Refers to thesis and topic sentences

■ Refers to supporting details

**Paragraph 1**

Chances are, your school has a student newspaper. School papers typically report on the goings-on around campus. *Cafeteria to Cease Selling Soft Drinks* might be the headline one week; *Track Team to Raise Funds for New Equipment* might appear the next. But occasionally, student-run papers publish a story that is so controversial it ends up being censored by the school administration. Such was the case in a midwestern high school in 2008. Both students and administrators learned lessons about the role of a school newspaper on campus, the authority of school administration, and the censorship of ideas.

How does the introductory paragraph set the stage for the event the author is reporting on?

### Paragraph 2

The story in question was written by junior Greta Barnoff, who investigated the practice of tracking in her suburban high school. Tracking is the practice of steering certain students toward more difficult classes (such as A.P. history or physics). Barnoff argued that the school was tacitly steering white students toward higher-level classes and steering minority students toward lower-level ones. Barnoff researched her article by comparing the test scores and classroom placement of the white and minority students in the school's junior class. To do this she used information published by the federal government under the No Child Left Behind Act.

### Paragraph 3

Make a list of everyone the author chose to quote. What do the speakers have in common? What is their relationship to the story at hand?

"I put together what I thought was a pretty clear exposé of the way the racial divide breaks down academically in our school," said Barnoff. "The numbers tell a clear story about the role race plays in the achievement gap." Barnoff said she hoped her article would get school administrators to address the problem of racism in the school.

### Paragraph 4

But before the story had a chance to run, it was pulled by the school's principal, Dr. Randell Evern. Evern said he could not allow the story to go to press because it inappropriately exposed the private information of students. Indeed, to make her point, Barnoff listed the specific grades and class choices alongside the names of members of the junior class.

### Paragraph 5

"I have an obligation to protect the privacy of our students," said Evern. "It is not, and has never been, the job of the school newspaper to post private information about individuals. Grades, test scores, and student schedules are pieces of private information that have no business being on the pages of any publication without an individual's consent."

What features of this essay let you know it is not a persuasive essay?

### Paragraph 6

When students opened their school paper, the *Beacon*, on Monday morning, they were greeted by a blank spread where Barnoff's story was supposed to be.

### Paragraph 7

Barnoff, a junior reporter for the paper, and Emily Smigel, the editor-in-chief, opposed Evern's decision to cut the story. Said Smigel, "I think the fact that Dr. Evern chose to censor the story is evidence of just how important it was to run it. The privacy issue is just a cover for them to hide behind."

### Paragraph 8

Yet other students appreciated Evern's efforts to protect their private information. Said one student, who asked that his name not be used: "I don't need people seeing that I got a C- in biology last semester. That's my business. The school did the right thing by protecting the students. The only way it would have been OK to publish it is if they [the reporters] were going to get the permission of every single student to publish their name and information."

This is Paragraph 8's topic sentence. It lets you know that this paragraph will discuss students who supported the principal's decision to censor the story.

### Paragraph 9

Another student pointed out that many school functions do not have the authority that they would in the real world. "The *Beacon* isn't, like, the *New York Times* or something,"

What point does this quote serve to support?

said sophomore Karen Blackmer. "It's just a student rag. Lots of stuff that goes on here at school isn't 'real.' Our class president doesn't have presidential authority—any decisions she makes are approved or overridden by the principal. It's the same way with the student newspaper. We're in school for practice, not for real life."

### Paragraph 10

But other students disagreed with the administration's decision to shield them from well-documented information and suspected it of trying to cover up a serious problem within the school. Said junior Matt DeBlasio, who takes photographs for the *Beacon*: "The article didn't discuss anything illegal or immoral. It didn't encourage students to do drugs or have sex or cheat or anything. It was a well-researched story. The fact that the administration pulled it only proves they have something to hide."

### Paragraph 11

What specific details are discussed in Paragraph 11?

To emphasize the point that his decision to censor the story was out of respect for students' private information, Dr. Evern said he would form a committee to investigate the claims made in the article, which has thus far been read only by the newspaper's editors, supervisors, and top-level school administrators. He invited concerned members of the student body to participate in a series of after-school discussions on the matter. "Certainly we welcome student input on this serious matter," he said.

### Paragraph 12

When writing a report, it is a good idea to conclude by letting your readers know where they can find more information on the subject.

Since the 2008 incident, no further incidents of censorship at the *Beacon* have occurred. For more information on censorship in schools, check out the Center for Campus Free Speech, on the Web at www.campusspeech.org.

## Works Cited

All interviews conducted by Friedman, Lauri S. 1–8 Oct. 2008.

# Exercise 3A: Conduct an Interview

Essay Three, "When Student Newspapers Are Censored: One School's Story," was written after conducting interviews with Greta Barnoff, Randell Evern, Emily Smigel, Matt DeBlasio, and several other people. When reporting on events that occur in your community, you will probably need to interview people to get critical information and opinions. Interviews allow you to get the story behind a participant's experiences, enabling you to provide a fuller picture of the event.

The key to a successful interview is asking the right questions. You want the respondent to answer in as much detail as possible so you can write an accurate, colorful, and interesting piece. Therefore, you should have a clear idea of what general pieces of information you want to find out from the respondent before you begin interviewing. The six classic journalist's questions —who, what, when, where, why, and how—are an excellent place to begin. If you get answers to each of these questions, you will end up with a pretty good picture of the event that took place.

Interviews can be conducted in many ways, but the following suggestions will help you get started:

**Step One. Choose a setting with little distraction.**
Avoid bright lights or loud noises, and make sure the person you are interviewing feels comfortable speaking to you. Professional settings such as offices, places of business, and homes are always appropriate settings for an interview. If it is a phone interview, be sure you can clearly hear what the person is saying (so do not conduct the interview on a cell phone while walking on a busy city block, for example).

**Step Two. Explain who you are and what you intend to learn from the interview.**
Identify yourself. For what publication are you writing? If you are writing for a school paper, identify the paper.

If you are conducting research for an ongoing project, explain the project's goals and in what way you expect the interviewee can help you reach them. Indicate how long you expect the interview to take, and get all contact information upfront.

**Step Three. Ask specific questions, and start at the beginning.**

Make sure you ask at least two questions that address each of the following ideas: who, what, where, when, why, and how. Who was involved in the event? What happened during the course of the event? Where did it take place? Specific questions will change depending on what type of event you are covering. Follow your instincts; if you do not know something or have a question, ask. The answer will likely yield good information that will enhance your report.

**Step Four. Take notes.**

Never rely on your memory when conducting an interview. Either type or jot down notes, or ask permission to tape or otherwise record the interview.

**Step Five. Verify quotes and information.**

Before you write your report, it is important to go back to your source to double-check key points of information. Also, you must run any quotes you intend to use by the source before you put them in your report. This is to make sure you heard the person accurately and are not misrepresenting his or her position.

## Types of Questions to Ask During an Interview

Questions you will ask your interviewees tend to fall into a few basic categories.

Knowledge: What do they know about the topic or event? This can include historical background, logistics, and outcomes of an event. For example, Greta Barnoff in Essay Three provided the interviewer with information about how she researched the article that was cut from her school paper.

**Sensory:** Ask questions about what people have seen, touched, heard, tasted, or smelled. These details will help your readers vividly imagine the event you are reporting on.

**Behavior:** What motivated the person to become involved in this project or movement? What does the person hope to gain by having his or her story publicized?

**Opinions, values, and feelings:** What does the person think about the topic or event? These questions result in opinionated or personal statements that you, as an objective reporter, most likely will not make in your report. For example, in Essay Three, the author quotes from students and administrators to express opinions on the event in a way that would be inappropriate for an objective reporter to do.

## Exercise 3B: Report on an Event

Reports show up in many publications—newspapers, magazines, journals, and web logs (blogs) are just some of the places people turn to to read about events and activities underway in their community. Think about the type of event you would like to report on. It could be a trip summary; the happenings of a local or school event, such as a parade, speech, assembly, or rally; a sports game; a party; or another experience in which people are coming together to get something done. Think next about the type of publication in which your report would best appear. Trip summaries, or travelogues, make great fodder for blogs; reports on school events such as sports games or performances are best featured in the school paper.

Before you report on an event, make sure you have done thorough research. Look over all notes from your interviews. Outline a road map for your essay to follow. (See exercises in this book on how to outline an essay prior to writing it.) Examine where quotations, information, and other details will fit best. After you absorb and organize all the information you have collected, you are ready to write.

News reports tend to be objective, so make sure your writing style is impartial and matter-of-fact. Also, be sure to provide the reader with enough information to visualize the event, but not so much that you bombard them with unnecessary or unrelated details. Use the other writing exercises found in this book—on using quotations, writing introductions and conclusions, and gathering research—to help you write the report. Then submit it for publication.

# Write Your Own Expository Five-Paragraph Essay

Using the information from this book, write your own five-paragraph expository essay that deals with a topic relating to censorship. You can use the resources in this book for information about issues relating to this topic and how to structure this type of essay.

The following steps are suggestions on how to get started.

**Step One: Choose your topic.**

The first step is to decide what topic to write your expository essay on. Is there any subject that particularly fascinates you? Is there an issue you strongly support or feel strongly against? Is there a topic you feel personally connected to or one that you would like to learn more about? Ask yourself such questions before selecting your essay topic. Refer to Appendix D: Sample Essay Topics if you need help selecting a topic.

**Step Two: Write down questions and answers about the topic.**

Before you begin writing, you will need to think carefully about what ideas your essay will contain. This is a process known as *brainstorming*. Brainstorming involves asking yourself questions and coming up with ideas to discuss in your essay. Possible questions that will help you with the brainstorming process include:

- Why is this topic important?
- Why should people be interested in this topic?
- How can I make this essay interesting to the reader?
- What question am I going to address in this paragraph or essay?
- What facts, ideas, or quotes can I use to support the answer to my question?

Questions especially for expository essays include:
- Do I want to write an informative essay or an opinionated essay?

- Will I need to explain a process or course of action?
- Will my essay contain many definitions or explanations?
- Is there a particular problem that needs to be solved?

### Step Three: Gather facts, ideas, and anecdotes related to your topic.

This book contains several places to find information, including the viewpoints and the appendixes. In addition, you may want to research the books, articles, and Web sites listed in Section Three or do additional research in your local library. You can also conduct interviews if you know someone who has a compelling story that would fit well in your essay.

### Step Four: Develop a workable thesis statement.

Use what you have written down in steps two and three to help you articulate the main point or argument you want to make in your essay. It should be expressed in a clear sentence and make an arguable or supportable point.

*Example:*

**China, a nation famous for its tight stranglehold on information, has an intricate process for censoring both print and electronic information.**

This could be the thesis statement of a process expository essay that explains how Chinese censors block information that appears in print sources and on the Internet.

### Step Five: Write an outline or diagram.

1. Write the thesis statement at the top of the outline.
2. Write roman numerals I, II, and III on the left side of the page with A, B, and C under each numeral.
3. Next to each roman numeral, write down the best ideas you came up with in step three. These should all directly relate to and support the thesis statement.

4. Next to each letter write down information that supports that particular idea.

**Step Six: Write the three supporting paragraphs.**
Use your outline to write the three supporting paragraphs. Write down the main idea of each paragraph in sentence form. Do the same thing for the supporting points of information. Each sentence should support the topic of the paragraph. Be sure you have relevant and interesting details, facts, and quotes. Use transitions when you move from idea to idea to keep the text fluid and smooth. Sometimes, although not always, paragraphs can include a concluding or summary sentence that restates the paragraph's argument.

**Step Seven: Write the introduction and conclusion.**
See Exercise 2B for information on writing introductions and conclusions.

**Step Eight: Read and rewrite.**
As you read, check your essay for the following:

✔ Does the essay maintain a consistent tone?

✔ Do all paragraphs reinforce your general thesis?

✔ Do all paragraphs flow from one to the other? Do you need to add transition words or phrases?

✔ Have you quoted from reliable, authoritative, and interesting sources?

✔ Is there a sense of progression throughout the essay?

✔ Does the essay get bogged down in too much detail or irrelevant material?

✔ Does your introduction grab the reader's attention?

✔ Does your conclusion reflect on any previous-ly discussed material or give the essay a sense of closure?

✔ Are there any spelling or grammatical errors?

# Section Three: Supporting Research Material

# Facts About Censorship

**Editor's Note:** These facts can be used in reports to reinforce or add credibility when making important points or claims.

## Free Speech and the Constitution

- Since 1791, the U.S. Constitution has protected freedom of speech from interference by the federal government.
- Free speech is protected by the First Amendment of the Bill of Rights.
- The text of the First Amendment reads: "Congress shall make no law respecting an establishment of religion, or prohibiting the free exercise thereof; or abridging the freedom of speech, or of the press; or the right of the people peaceably to assemble, and to petition the government for a redress of grievances."
- Freedom of speech was first challenged seven years after the First Amendment was ratified. In an effort to reduce and silence opposition to an expected war with France, the Sedition Act of 1798 was passed. This made it illegal to speak or write against the government.
- The Sedition Act expired in 1801 and was not renewed.
- In the United States, National Freedom of Speech Week is celebrated during the third week of October each year.

## Free Speech and the Supreme Court

The Supreme Court has ruled on over 125 First Amendment cases.

The first case was heard in 1919, in *Schenck v. United States*. The Court ruled that the federal government can restrict free speech if the speech presents a "clear and present danger" to the nation.

Other key Supreme Court free speech cases have included:

- *Chaplinsky v. New Hampshire* (1942): rules that some words are not protected under the First Amendment because they are equivalent to violent actions.
- *Roth v. United States* (1957): rules that obscene material is not protected by the First Amendment.
- *Stanley v. Georgia* (1964): Personal possession of obscene material in a citizen's house may not be prohibited by law; upheld in *Ashcroft v. Free Speech Coalition* (2002).
- *Brandenburg v. Ohio* (1969): A case involving a Ku Klux Klan leader's right to free speech causes the Court to rule that speech can be restricted only if it incites "imminent lawless action."
- *Tinker v. Des Moines Independent Community School District* (1969): rules that the First Amendment protects a student's right to wear armbands as part of a legitimate protest.
- *Cohen v. California* (1971): rules that a person cannot be convicted for wearing clothing that bears obscenities in a courtroom.
- *Miller v. California* (1973): rules that in order to be deemed obscene, speech must have "no redeeming social value."
- *Hazelwood v. Kuhlmeier* (1988): rules that public school student newspapers are subject to a lower level of First Amendment protection than a variety of other student and nonstudent publications.
- *Texas v. Johnson* (1989): finds that citizens cannot be prosecuted for desecrating the American flag.
- *Barnes v. Glen Theatre, Inc.* (1991): rules that nude dancing is not protected by the First Amendment.
- *Reno v. ACLU* (1997): rules that the Communications Decency Act, which regulates certain content

on the Internet, is too broad and thus is an uncon-stitutional restraint on the First Amendment.

- *Cuffley v. Mickes* (1999): rules that the Ku Klux Klan should be allowed to sponsor an Adopt-A-Highway program as would any other organization.
- *United States v. Williams* (2008): rules that prohibiting offers to provide and requests to obtain child pornography does not violate the First Amendment.
- *Morse v. Frederick* (2008): rules it was appropriate for school administrators to discipline students for displaying a banner that read "Bong Hits 4 Jesus" at a school-sponsored event.

## Opinions About Censorship and Free Speech

According to online surveys conducted by the GVU Center at the Georgia Institute of Technology's College of Computing:

- 24.84 percent of Americans "agree strongly" that certain information should not be published on the Internet.
- 22.30 percent of Americans "agree somewhat" that certain information should not be published on the Internet.
- 9.23 percent neither agree nor disagree.
- 15.26 percent disagree somewhat.
- 28.37 percent disagree strongly.

A 2005 national poll by Hostway found that:

- 52 percent of respondents believe bloggers should benefit from the same First Amendment rights and protections as professional journalists.
- 21 percent disagree.
- 80 percent believe bloggers should not have the right to publish home addresses and other personal information about private citizens.
- 72 percent believe bloggers should not have the right to publish home addresses or other personal

information about public figures (such as celebrities or sport figures).

- 68 percent believe bloggers should not have the right to publish home addresses or other personal information about appointed government officials (such as judges or mayors).

A poll conducted by the Pew Internet and American Life Project from 2000 through 2007 found the following opinions of Chinese Internet censorship:

- More than 80 percent of Chinese citizens think the Internet should be managed or controlled in some way.
- 87 percent of Internet users would control or manage pornography.
- 86 percent would want violent content controlled or managed.
- 83 percent would want spam or junk mail controlled or managed.
- 66 percent would want advertisements controlled or managed.
- 64 percent would want slander against individuals controlled or managed.
- 50 percent would want online gaming controlled or managed.
- 41 percent would want online political content controlled or managed.
- 27 percent would want online chatting controlled or managed.
- 85 percent believe the Chinese government should be responsible for controlling or managing online content.
- 79 percent said Internet companies should be responsible for controlling or managing online content.
- 68 percent said parents should be responsible for controlling or managing online content.
- 64 percent said schools should be responsible for controlling or managing online content.

- 59 percent said Internet cafés should be responsible for controlling or managing online content.

A 2007 British Broadcasting Company survey of 11,344 people in fourteen countries revealed a world divided about the importance of free speech in the press:

- 56 percent of those interviewed thought that freedom of the press was very important to ensure a free society.
- 40 percent said it was more important to maintain social harmony and peace, even if it meant curbing the press's freedom to report news truthfully.

# Finding and Using Sources of Information

No matter what type of essay you are writing, it is necessary to find information to support your point of view. You can use sources such as books, magazine articles, newspaper articles, and online articles.

## Using Books and Articles

You can find books and articles in a library by using the library's computer or cataloging system. If you are not sure how to use these resources, ask a librarian to help you. You can also use a computer to find many magazine articles and other articles written specifically for the Internet.

You are likely to find a lot more information than you can possibly use in your essay, so your first task is to narrow it down to what is likely to be most usable. Look at book and article titles. Look at book chapter titles, and examine the book's index to see if it contains information on the specific topic you want to write about. (For example, if you want to write about censorship of the Internet in other countries and you find a book about China, check the chapter titles and index to be sure it contains information about Internet censorship before you bother to check out the book.)

For a five-paragraph essay, you do not need a great deal of supporting information, so quickly try to narrow down your materials to a few good books and magazine or Internet articles. You do not need dozens. You might even find that one or two good books or articles contain all the information you need.

You probably do not have time to read an entire book, so find the chapters or sections that relate to your topic, and skim these. When you find useful information, copy it onto a note card or notebook. You should look for supporting facts, statistics, quotations, and examples.

## Using the Internet

When you select your supporting information, it is important that you evaluate its source. This is especially important with information you find on the Internet. Because nearly anyone can put information on the Internet, there is as much bad information as good information. Before using Internet information—or any information— try to determine if the source seems to be reliable. Is the author or Internet site sponsored by a legitimate organization? Is it from a government source? Does the author have any special knowledge or training relating to the topic you are looking up? Does the article give any indication of where its information comes from?

## Using Your Supporting Information

When you use supporting information from a book, article, interview, or other source, there are three important things to remember:

1. *Make it clear whether you are using a direct quotation or a paraphrase.* If you copy information directly from your source, you are quoting it. You must put quotation marks around the information and tell where the information comes from. If you put the information in your own words, you are paraphrasing it.

*Here is an example of a using a quotation:*
Trying to censor the Internet using filter programs that block inappropriate Web sites is not a good way to prevent children from viewing them. As author Fred Reed reports, "Automated censorship invariably ends up blocking much that it shouldn't." (C11)

*Here is an example of a brief paraphrase of the same passage:*
Trying to censor the Internet using filter programs that block inappropriate Web sites is not a good

way to prevent children from viewing them. Such programs usually end up blocking content that is not necessarily objectionable—an auto block on the search term "sex," for example, might also block Web sites about sex education, STD prevention, and condom use, important subjects for young people to be able to research.

2. *Use the information fairly.* Be careful to use supporting information in the way the author intended it. For example, it is unfair to quote an author as saying, "Terrorists should have the right to say whatever they want" when he or she intended to say, "Terrorists should have the right to say whatever they want—provided they are discussing topics that don't incite other people to mass murder." This is called taking information out of context. This is using supporting evidence unfairly.

3. *Give credit where credit is due.* Giving credit is known as citing. You must use citations when you use someone else's information, but not every piece of supporting information needs a citation.

   - If the supporting information is general knowledge —that is, it can be found in many sources— you do not have to cite your source.
   - If you directly quote a source, you must cite it.
   - If you paraphrase information from a specific source, you must cite it.

If you do not use citations where you should, you are *plagiarizing*—or stealing—someone else's work.

## Citing Your Sources

There are a number of ways to cite your sources. Your teacher will probably want you to do it in one of three ways:

- Informal: As in the example in number 1 above, tell where you got the information as you present it in the text of your essay.

- Informal list: At the end of your essay, place an unnumbered list of all the sources you used. This tells the reader where, in general, your information came from.
- Formal: Use numbered footnotes. Footnotes are generally placed at the end of an article or essay, although they may be placed elsewhere depending on your teacher's requirements.

## Works Cited

Reed, Fred. "Should Online Porn Be Barred?" *Washington Times* 5 Jan. 2008: C11.

# Using MLA Style to Create a Works Cited List

You will probably need to create a list of works cited for your paper. These include materials that you quoted from, relied heavily on, or consulted to write your paper. There are several different ways to structure these references. The following examples are based on Modern Language Association (MLA) style, one of the major citation styles used by writers.

## Book Entries

For most book entries you will need the author's name, the book's title, where it was published, what company published it, and the year it was published. This information is usually found on the inside of the book. Variations on book entries include the following:

*A book by a single author:*
Friedman, Thomas. *Hot, Flat, and Crowded: Why We Need a Green Revolution—and How It Can Renew America.* New York: Farrar, Straus and Giroux, 2008.

*Two or more books by the same author:*
Pollen, Michael. *Botany of Desire: A Plant's-Eye View of the World.* New York: Random House, 2002.

———. *The Omnivore's Dilemma: A Natural History of Four Meals.* New York: Penguin Books, 2006.

*A book by two or more authors:*
Esposito, John L., and Dalia Mogahed. *Who Speaks for Islam? What a Billion Muslims Really Think.* Washington, DC: Gallup Press, 2008.

*A book with an editor:*
> Skancke, Jennifer S., ed. *Introducing Issues with Opposing Viewpoints: Stem Cell Research*. Detroit: Greenhaven, 2008.

## Periodical and Newspaper Entries

Entries for sources found in periodicals and newspapers are cited a bit differently from books. For one, these sources usually have a title and a publication name. They also may have specific dates and page numbers. Unlike book entries, you do not need to list where newspapers or periodicals are published or what company publishes them.

*An article from a periodical:*
> Aldhous, Peter. "China's Burning Ambition. *Nature* 30 June 2005: 1152–55.

*An unsigned article from a periodical:*
> "Contraception in Middle School?" *Harvard Crimson* 21 Oct. 2007.

*An article from a newspaper:*
> Cunningham, Roseanna. "Care, Not Euthanasia, Is the Answer to the 'Problem' of the Elderly." *Sunday Times* [London] 20 July 2008: 21.

## Internet Sources

To document a source you found online, try to provide as much information on it as possible, including the author's name, the title of the document, date of publication or of last revision, the URL, and your date of access.

*A Web source:*
> Mieszkowski, Katharine. "Plastic Bags Are Killing Us." Salon.com 10 Aug. 2007. 9 Sept. 2008 < http://www.salon.com/news/feature/2007/08/10/plastic_bags/index.html > .

Your teacher will tell you exactly how information should be cited in your essay. Generally, the very least information needed is the original author's name and the name of the article or other publication.

Be sure you know exactly what information your teacher requires before you start looking for your supporting information so that you know what information to include with your notes.

# Sample Essay Topics

Free Speech Has Limits

Free Speech Should Have No Limits

Censorship Is Undemocratic

Moderate Censorship Can Exist Within a Democracy

Terrorist Speech Should Be Censored

Terrorist Speech Should Not Be Censored

The Internet Should Be Censored

The Internet Should Not Be Censored

Obscene Art Should Be Censored

Obscene Art Should Not Be Censored

Burning the American Flag Is Free Speech

Burning the American Flag Should Not Qualify
    as Free Speech

Pornography Should Be Covered by the First
    Amendment

Pornography Should Not Be Covered by the First
    Amendment

Explicit Song Lyrics Should Be Censored

Explicit Song Lyrics Should Not Be Censored

Violent Images on the News Should Be Censored

Violent Images on the News Should Not Be Censored

School Administrators Should Have the Final Say on
    Student Publications

School Administrators Should Not Have the Final Say
    on Student Publications

## Topics Specifically for Expository Essays

Examining What Qualifies as Obscene

The Limits of Free Speech in a School Environment

The Definition of Free Speech

How Censorship Threatens Democracy

Who Is Qualified to Be a Censor?

Exploring the Communications Decency Act

How American Companies Help China Censor

9/11 and Censorship: How the War on Terror
Has Affected Free Speech in America

# Organizations to Contact

The editors have compiled the following list of organizations concerned with the issues debated in this book. The descriptions are derived from materials provided by the organizations. All have publications or information available for interested readers. The list was compiled on the date of publication of the present volume; names, addresses, and phone numbers may change. Be aware that many organizations take several weeks or longer to respond to inquiries, so allow as much time as possible.

### American Civil Liberties Union (ACLU)
125 Broad St., 18th Flr., New York, NY 10004
(212) 549-2500 • fax: (212) 549-2646
e-mail: aclu@aclu.org • Web site: www.aclu.org

The ACLU opposes regulation of all forms of speech, including pornography and hate speech. The ACLU offers numerous reports, fact sheets, and policy statements on a wide variety of free speech and First Amendment issues.

### American Library Association (ALA)
50 E. Huron St., Chicago, IL 60611
(800) 545-2433 • fax: (312) 440-9374
e-mail: ala@ala.org • Web site: www.ala.org

The ALA is the nation's primary professional organization for librarians. Through its Office for Intellectual Freedom, the ALA supports free access to libraries and library materials. The OIF also monitors and opposes efforts to ban books.

### Canadian Association for Free Expression (CAFE)
PO Box 332 Station 'B'
Etobicoke, ON
CANADA M9W 5L3

(905) 897-7221
e-mail: cafe@canadafirst.net
Web site: www.canadianfreespeech.com

CAFE is one of Canada's leading civil liberties groups. It works to strengthen the freedom of speech and freedom of expression provisions in the Canadian Charter of Rights and Freedoms. It lobbies politicians and researches threats to freedom of speech. Publications include specialized reports, leaflets, and the *Free Speech Monitor*, which is published ten times a year.

## Center for Campus Free Speech
407 S. Dearborn St., Ste. 701
Chicago, IL 60605
(312) 291-0396
e-mail: center@campusspeech.org
Web site: www.campusspeech.org

Center for Campus Free Speech was created by a variety of members of the higher education community—students, faculty, administrators, and others—to protect and to promote free speech on campuses. The center acts as a clearinghouse of information; provides specialized support to campuses; and connects concerned educators, administrators, lawyers, and students into a national network. The center draws advice and guidance from a group of leaders in the higher education and legal communities.

## Electronic Frontier Foundation (EFF)
454 Shotwell St., San Francisco, CA 94110-1914
(415) 436-9333 • e-mail: information@eff.org
Web site: www.eff.org

EFF works to protect privacy and freedom of expression on the Internet. It deals with cutting-edge issues, including free speech, privacy, innovation, digital rights, and consumer rights. Its main priority is to protect digital freedom in all forms.

### The Free Expression Policy Project

170 W. Seventy-sixth St., #301, New York, NY 10023
e-mail: margeheins@verizon.net
Web site: www.fepproject.org

The Free Expression Policy Project, founded in 2000, provides research and advocacy on free speech, copyright, and media democracy issues. Its issues of interest include restrictions on publicly funded expression; Internet filters, rating systems, and other measures that restrict access to information and ideas in the digital age; restrictive copyright laws, digital rights management, and other imbalances in the intellectual property system; mass media consolidation, public access to the airwaves, and other issues of media democracy; and censorship designed to shield adolescents and children from controversial art, information, and ideas.

### Free Speech Coalition

PO Box 10480, Canoga Park, CA 91309
(800) 845-8503 or (818) 348-9373
e-mail: freespeech@pacificnet.net
Web site: www.freespeechcoalition.com

The coalition is a trade association that represents members of the adult entertainment industry. It seeks to protect the industry from attempts to censor pornography. Publications include fact sheets, *Free Speech X-Press*, and the report *The Truth About the Adult Entertainment Industry*.

### Freedom Forum

555 Pennsylvania Ave. NW
Washington, DC 20001
(202) 292-6100
e-mail: news@freedomforum.org
Web site: www.freedomforum.org

The Freedom Forum is dedicated to free press, free speech, and free spirit for all people. The foundation focuses on three priorities: the Newseum, First Amendment freedoms, and newsroom diversity.

## International Freedom of Expression Exchange (IFEX)

555 Richmond St. West, Ste. 1101
PO Box #407, Toronto, ON
CANADA M5V 3B 1
(416) 515-9622
e-mail: ifex@ifex.org • Web site: www.ifex.org

IFEX consists of more than forty organizations that support the freedom of expression. It claims to play a key role in addressing threats to free expression by exposing violations and raising awareness of the dangers faced by individuals in many countries who report the news or criticize powerful figures.

## Morality in Media (MIM)

475 Riverside Dr., Ste. 239, New York, NY 10115
(212) 870-3222
e-mail: mim@moralityinmedia.org
Web site: www.moralityinmedia.org

Morality in Media is an interfaith organization that fights obscenity and opposes indecency in the mainstream media. It believes pornography harms society. MIM maintains the National Obscenity Law Center, a clearinghouse of legal materials on obscenity law.

## National Coalition Against Censorship (NCAC)

275 Seventh Ave., New York, NY 10001
(212) 807-6222
e-mail: ncac@ncac.org • Web site: www.ncac.org

Founded in 1974, NCAC is an alliance of fifty national nonprofit organizations, including literary, artistic, religious, educational, professional, labor, and civil liberties groups. United by a conviction that freedom of thought, inquiry, and expression must be defended, it works to educate its members and the public at large about the dangers of censorship and how to oppose them.

## National Coalition for the Protection of Children and Families
800 Compton Rd., Ste. 9224
Cincinnati, OH 45231-9964
(513) 521-6227 • fax: (513) 521-6337
Web site: www.nationalcoalition.org

This is an organization of business, religious, and civic leaders who work to eliminate pornography. It encourages citizens to support the enforcement of obscenity laws and to close down neighborhood pornography outlets.

## OpenTheGovernment.org
1742 Connecticut Ave. NW, 3rd Flr.
Washington, DC 20009
(202) 332-OPEN (6736)
e-mail: info@openthegovernment.org
Web site: http://openthegovernment.org

OpenTheGovernment.org is a coalition of journalists, consumer and good-government groups, environmentalists, library groups, laborers, and others united to make the federal government more open and transparent.

## People for the American Way (PFAW)
2000 M St. NW, Ste. 400
Washington, DC 20036
(202) 467-4999 or (800) 326-PFAW (7329)
fax: (202) 293-2672
e-mail: pfaw@pfaw.org • Web site: www.pfaw.org

PFAW works to promote citizen participation in democracy and safeguard the principles of the U.S. Constitution, including the right to free speech. It publishes a variety of fact sheets, articles, and position statements on its Web site and distributes the e-mail newsletter *Freedom to Learn Online*.

## The Thomas Jefferson Center for the Protection of Free Expression

400 Worrell Dr., Charlottesville, VA 22911-8691
(434) 295-4784
Web site: www.tjcenter.org

The Thomas Jefferson Center for the Protection of Free Expression is devoted to the defense of free expression in all its forms. It sponsors a wide range of programs in education and the arts and active participation in judicial and legislative matters involving free expression. Each year on or near April 13 (the anniversary of the birth of Thomas Jefferson) the center focuses national attention on especially egregious or ridiculous affronts to free expression by awarding Jefferson Muzzles to responsible individuals or organizations. The center also recognizes those who have shown extraordinary devotion to the principles of free expression through its William J. Brennan Jr. Award.

## The Tully Center for Free Speech

S.I. Newhouse School of Public Communications
Syracuse University
215 University Pl., Syracuse, NY 13244-2100
(315) 443-4054
e-mail: befought@syr.edu
Web site: http//tully.syr.edu

The Tully Center for Free Speech is housed at Syracuse University's S.I. Newhouse School of Public Communications, one of the nation's premier schools of mass communications. The school prepares students for careers ranging from print journalism to broadcast journalism to online communication and from advertising and public relations to photography, graphics, and television production. The center encourages teaching and research about media law and free-speech issues and honors communicators who face free-speech threats.

# Bibliography

## Books

Byrd, Cathy, and Susan Richmond, eds., *Potentially Harmful: The Art of American Censorship*. Atlanta: Georgia State University, 2006.

Caso, Frank, *Global Issues: Censorship*. New York: Facts On File, 2008.

Couvares, Francis G., ed., *Movie Censorship and American Culture*. Amherst: University of Massachusetts Press, 2006.

Drewett, Michael, and Martin Cloonan, eds., *Popular Music Censorship in Africa*. Hampshire, UK: Ashgate, 2006.

Heins, Marjorie, *Not in Front of the Children: Indecency, Censorship, and the Innocence of Youth*. New Brunswick, NJ: Rutgers University Press, 2007.

Herumin, Wendy, *Censorship on the Internet: From Filters to Freedom of Speech*. Berkeley Heights, NJ: Enslow, 2004.

Korpe, Marie, ed., *Shoot the Singer! Music Censorship Today*. London: Zed, 2004.

## Periodicals

Bernstein, Richard, "What Is Free Speech, and What Is Terrorism?" *New York Times*, August 14, 2005. www.nytimes.com/2005/08/14/weekinreview/14imam.html.

Citizens for Families, "Garbage In . . . Garbage Out," 2004. www.strengthenthefamily.net/media/garbage_in_out_2004.pdf.

*Columbian* [Vancouver, WA], "In Our View: Internet Censor," May 7, 2008.

Committee on Homeland Security and Governmental Affairs, "Lieberman Calls on Google to Take Down Terrorist Content," May 19, 2008. http://hsgac.sen

ate.gov/public/index.cfm?Fuseaction = PressReleases. Detail&PressReleaseid = 8093d5b2-c882-4d12-883d-5c670d43d269&Month = 5&Year = 2008.

*Daily Sentinel* [Grand Junction, Co], "Parents Must Filter Internet, Not Censors," May 1, 2008.

Dietrich, Tamara, "Censoring Winner of Student Art Show Is in Poor Taste," *Daily Press*, April 9, 2008.

Fein, Bruce, "Tackling a Root Cause of Terrorism," *Washington Times*, December 21, 2004.

Finkelstein, Seth, "The Internet Can't Be Censored and It's Wrong for Governments to Try," *Guardian* (Manchester, UK), September 13, 2007. www.guardian.co.uk/technol ogy/2007/sep/13/guardianweeklytechnologysection. comment.

Finkelstein, Seth, "Technology: Read Me First: If You Block Online Porn, You'll Surely Block Dissent in China," *Guardian* (Manchester, UK), April 17, 2008.

French, David, "A Bong Hit to Free Speech," *National Review*, June 25, 2007.

Heins, Marjorie, Christina Cho, and Ariel Feldman, "Internet Filters: A Public Policy Report," Brennan Center for Justice, 2006. www. fepproject.org/poli cyreports/filters2.pdf.

Kaiser Family Foundation, "See No Evil: How Internet Filters Affect the Search for Online Health Information," 2002. www.kaisernetwork.org/health_cast/uploaded_ files/Internet_Filtering_exec_summ.pdf.

Kimmage, Daniel, "Fight Terror with YouTube," *New York Times*, June 26, 2008. www.nytimes.com/2008/06/26/ opinion/26kimmage.html?pagewanted = print.

Levy, Janet, "The Erosion of Free Speech," FrontPageMagazine.com, July 4, 2008. http://front pagemag.com/Articles/Read.aspx?GUID = 1CAC2897-674D-44AB-ADF4-BA77930F421E.

Liptak, Adam, "Hate Speech or Free Speech? What Much of West Bans Is Protected in U.S.," *International*

*Herald Tribune*, June 11, 2008. www.iht.com/articles/2008/06/11/america/hate.php.

McCarthy, Andrew C., "Free Speech for Terrorists?" *Commentary*, March 2005. www.commentarymagazine.com/viewarticle.cfm/free-speech-for-terrorist--9864.

McLaughlin, Kathleen E., "China's Model for a Censored Internet," *Christian Science Monitor*, September 22, 2005. www.csmonitor.com/2005/0922/po1s02-woap.html.

*New York Sun*, "Free Speech of the Times," May 30, 2008. www.nysun.com/editorials/free-speech-of-the-times/78979.

*New York Times*, "Joe Lieberman, Would-Be Censor," May 25, 2008. www.nytimes.com/2008/05/25/opinion/25sun1.html.

Reed, Fred, "Should Online Porn Be Barred?" *Washington Times*, January 5, 2008.

Reed, Fred, "Slippery Slope of a Web Censor," *Washington Times*, October 27, 2007.

Soupcoff, Marni, "Mark Freiman Makes the Case for Censoring Hate," *National Post*, May 21, 2008.

Thompson, Bill, "Which Freedoms Do We Want Online?" BBC.com, May 23, 2007. http://news.bbc.co.uk/2/hi/technology/6685253.stm.

Thompson, Bill, "Why Google in China Makes Sense," British Broadcasting Company, January 27, 2006. http://news.bbc.co.uk/1/hi/technology/4654014.stm.

Wilson, John K., "The Case of the Censored Newspaper," *Inside Higher Ed*, June 24, 2005. www.insidehighered.com/views/2005/06/24/wilson.

## Web Sites

**Electronic Privacy Information Center** (http://epic.org). EPIC is a public interest research center in Washington, D.C. It was established in 1994 to focus public attention on emerging civil liberties issues and to protect privacy, the First Amendment, and constitutional values. Its Web site contains links to breaking news related to the First Amendment and to reports published by the center.

**Free Expression** (www.cdt.org/speech). This page, run by the Center for Democracy and Technology, links to valuable, credible resources on the Communications Decency Act (CDA), the Child Online Protection Act (COPA), political speech, spam, net neutrality, and more.

**Free Speech Coalition** (www.freespeechcoalition.org). Founded in 1993, the Free Speech Coalition is a nonpartisan group of ideologically diverse nonprofit organizations and the for-profit organizations that help them raise funds and implement programs. Its mission is to protect the First Amendment rights of nonprofits and reduce or eliminate the excessive regulatory burdens they face. Contains useful primary source documents and articles.

**Free Speech Radio News** (www.fsrn.org). This is the Web site of a grassroots, worker-run radio news program that provides links to news stories and audio files.

**National Freedom of Speech Week** (www.freespeechweek.org). This site is geared toward encouraging schools, organizations, and communities across the country to commemorate National Freedom of Speech Week (NFSW), which occurs annually in October.

**Youth Free Expression Network** (www.ncac.org/YFEN/index.cfm). This national coalition of teens and adults is committed to defending the free expression rights of youth. YFEN's goal is to empower youth to advocate on their own behalf. It rejects censorial measures enacted in the presumed interest of "protecting" youth from critical information on subjects ranging from human rights and feminism to drugs and safer sex.

# Index

# Picture Credits

AP Images, 51

Dennis Brack/Bloomberg News/Landov, 20, 53

Scott J. Ferrell/Congressional Quarterly/Getty Images, 24

Alexis C. Glenn/UPI/Landov, 30

Hulton Archive/Getty Images, 61

Image copyright Jason Maehl, 2008. Used under license from shutterstock.com, 27

Patrick D. McDermott/UPI/Landov, 39

© Ed Quinn/Corbis, 57

Jewel Samad/AFP/Getty Images, 35

© Mike Segar/Reuters/Corbis, 11

Jeff Topping/Getty Images, 17

© Rob Wilkinson/Alamy, 8

Stefan Zaklin/Getty Images, 43

Steve Zmina, 9, 12, 32, 40, 52, 58–59

# About the Editor

Lauri S. Friedman earned her bachelor's degree in religion and political science from Vassar College in Poughkeepsie, New York. Her studies there focused on political Islam. Friedman has worked as a nonfiction writer, a newspaper journalist, and an editor for more than eight years. She has extensive experience in both academic and professional writing settings.

Friedman is the founder of LSF Editorial, a writing and editing business in San Diego. Her clients include Greenhaven Press, for whom she has edited and authored numerous publications on controversial social issues such as oil, the Internet, the Middle East, democracy, pandemics, and obesity. Every book in the *Writing the Critical Essay* series has been under her direction or editorship, and she has personally written more than eighteen titles in the series. She was instrumental in the creation of the series and played a critical role in its conception and development.